SUBLIME MARLENE

SUBLIME MARLENE

Thierry de Navacelle

Photographs from
the Kobal Collection

Translated from the French by
Carey L. Smith

SIDGWICK & JACKSON
LONDON

First published in Great Britain in 1984
by Sidgwick and Jackson Limited
First softcover edition 1985

Originally published in France in 1982 by Editions Ramsay
Copyright © Editions Ramsay, Paris, 1982
Translation copyright © 1984 by Sidgwick and Jackson Limited, London

Acknowledgements:
    Christine Tcherniak, Jean-Paul Iommi,
    Jacques Chevalier, Claude de Montremy

Picture Credits:
    Cinémathèque Française, 40
    Keystone, 135, 137
    MAGNUM, 138
    Paris-Match, 136
    Roger-Viollet, 150
    SIPA PRESS, 134, 137, 139
    All other photographs come from
    the Kobal Collection

Photographers' Acknowledgements:
    Kenneth Alexander, 18
    Davis Boulton, 126
    Don English, 43, 48, 75, 76 below
    John Engstead, 97, 132, 143
    Gragnon, 136
    Robert Hawkins, 125
    Ray Jones, 92, 102 left, 102 right, 106 below
    Lipnitzki, 150
    Eugène Robert Richee, 10, 11 left, 11 right,
        16 left, 16 right, 17, 79

Text credit:
    The extract on page 38 is taken from the screenplay of
    Morocco published by Lorrimer Publishers, London, 1972

ISBN: 0–283–99042–2 (Hardcover)
ISBN: 0–283–99043–0 (Softcover)

Phototypeset by Falcon Graphic Art Ltd,
Wallington, Surrey
Printed in Great Britain by
Biddles Limited, Guildford, Surrey
for Sidgwick and Jackson Limited,
1 Tavistock Chambers, Bloomsbury Way,
London WC1A 2SG

CONTENTS

INTRODUCTION

Beauty comes from within.
The idea might seem horrible but it's true.

MARLENE DIETRICH

The Sublime comes from the heart, and has nothing
to do with the mind ....

HONORE DE BALZAC

One evening in 1975 *Morocco* was playing at the
Film Institute in Los Angeles, and I was in the audience. Right from
the opening sequence I was enthralled: avidly I watched the long
shot of the mule refusing to move, with the legionnaires in the
background; Gary Cooper and the Arab women; and Marlene,
looking forlorn, emerging out of the fog on the deck of a steamer,
with Adolphe Menjou watching her. With a few precise, economical
shots, Josef von Sternberg managed to transport us into another
world. The characters were introduced and the plot outlined, so
that he could speak to us through his images. My fascination with
Marlene Dietrich stems from that day.

What struck me most the first time I saw *Morocco* was something
that was to prove more and more apparent: in her private life, as
well as in her films, Marlene has always displayed a constant zest
for living, great humanity and amazing generosity. As far as possible
I have seen all her films and read everything that could have been
written about her or by her, and have discovered a highly engaging
personality.

This book makes no claims to be exhaustive: what it does attempt
is to convey the magic experienced when watching Marlene on the
screen. It also takes a further admiring look at the life of this
extraordinary personality, for her career must rate as one of the
most varied that Hollywood has ever known.

*Morocco, 1930. Amy Jolly
(Marlene Dietrich) on board
ship, looking through the fog*

DIETRICH THE WOMAN

**I don't see how you could say that I play a game in my private life.
To do that, I would have to pretend to be something that I am not,
something false, something that somebody else would expect me to be.**
MARLENE DIETRICH

Above all else Marlene is totally feminine, in the widest sense of the word. Of course, one cannot completely dismiss the 'Marlene myth' or the fact that von Sternberg is partly responsible for it. But, as he says himself in his autobiography, *Fun in a Chinese Laundry*, he only 'dramatized her attributes'; he created nothing that did not exist already. Marlene made use of this myth to create a kind of protective barrier around herself, and so maintained her *femme fatale* image throughout her life.

The myth started in the early 1930s when Marlene arrived in Hollywood. Paramount's publicity machine, under von Sternberg's supervision, had taken things in hand: she had to lose 33 lb, take English lessons, and enshroud her past in a veil of mystery; wild rumours promptly began to circulate.

The idea was to create a new Garbo, but it was quickly abandoned when everyone saw how, in *The Blue Angel, Morocco* and *Dishonored*, Marlene succeeded in projecting her own personality. However, unlike some other actresses, Marlene knew how to keep her identity. Transcending artifice, she has gone on and on confirming this ability, which is why her career has lasted so long and why her fans have never been disappointed. 'Beauty comes from within,' she said. Marlene's beauty at the age of eighty is the best possible proof that her beauty at the age of thirty was anything but superficial.

'Erotic' is an adjective often used to describe Marlene. I prefer not to over-emphasize this aspect of her personality – though that does not mean that it can be ignored or that it did not play an important part in her career. But it is perhaps more novel to assess the human side of her character.

Marlene is a woman in every sense. She is both mother and child, both a woman who loves luxury and an efficient housewife. Tough but vulnerable, she feels a strong need for protection. She is independent and liberated, but she clings to her principles and maintains a certain conservatism. This duality, this ambiguity, which comes across in all her films, makes her a character who never ceases to surprise us.

In *Blonde Venus* von Sternberg exploited this to the full by making Marlene a devoted mother as well as a beguiling cabaret singer. Every great director who has worked with her, notably Billy Wilder in *Witness for the Prosecution* and Alfred Hitchcock in *Stage Fright*, has played on this ambiguity to lend piquancy to his screenplay.

The task of highlighting the qualities of such a personality is greatly facilitated by Marlene's outward sensitivity. Von Sternberg taught her not just how to make the most of it but how to turn such sensitivity into an explosive force. Von Sternberg's films reveal something which those of other directors lack; under him, Marlene was able on screen to charge the most basic

*Maria Magdalene Dietrich,
aged about four, taken by the
Imperial court photographer
in 1905*

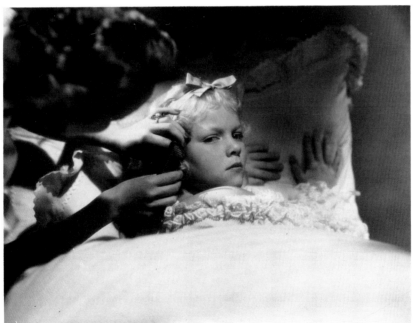

Above: About the time of The Devil is a Woman, *1935*

Left: Maria Sieber, aged about eight, playing her mother as a child in The Scarlet Empress, *1934*

human emotions with incredible intensity. She possessed the ability to convey despair, ecstasy, inner anguish and passion, as well as shyness, modesty, and even abstract attitudes like responsibility and resignation.

Take, for example, this scene from *Morocco*. Marlene, having discreetly slipped the key of her bedroom to Gary Cooper, gives him a disconcertingly tepid reception. The stratagem of a woman who, having attempted to seduce a man, refuses to give herself to him, who allows him finally to leave and then goes in search of him in the streets, might seem banal and uninteresting at first sight. And yet von Sternberg instils such tension, and Marlene such intensity of feeling, that the scene is given quite another dimension. Marlene's attitude changes from one moment to the next: she oscillates between the blasé and the naïve. Her face registers in turn weariness, scorn, total abandon, and irony. Gary Cooper, playing opposite her as if butter wouldn't melt in his mouth, only serves to underscore this complexity of character (see photographs on pages 12 and 13, and extract from screenplay on page 38). The swift transition from one extreme of mood to the next gives this scene its impetus. The same is true of the rest of *Morocco* and, generally, for most of the seven films von Sternberg and Dietrich made together.

Many people, simplifying the matter, have labelled von Sternberg a romantic. Today romanticism is synonymous with melancholy, idealism, and utopia. However, Marlene's energy and von Sternberg's depth of character do not fit this definition. Originally romanticism was the language of the soul, and the human soul is much too sensitive and complex to let itself be confined within such a semantic strait-jacket.

Strengthened by her work with von Sternberg, Marlene has continued to play intelligently on these fluxes of mood and on her sensitivity. She has never failed to attach great importance to being emotionally honest, as Sternberg had taught her to be.

If we wonder why some products of the Actors' Studio fail to convince us, it is no doubt because their emotions are 'fabricated' and unreal – they hide behind their roles. They cry but their tears are not genuine: they are only the tears of the character. When Marlene has tears in her eyes as she leaves John Wayne in *Seven Sinners* we feel it really is she who is crying. The credit goes to both Tay Garnett, as director, and Marlene.

Even when she is imperfectly directed, for example in Henry Koster's *No Highway*, Marlene knows how to stir her audience's feelings. She does this by playing astutely on the personality of her characters. When an apparently cold, hard, and sophisticated woman appears upset and suddenly confused, the impact is that much greater. We are reminded again here of Billy Wilder's *Witness for the Prosecution*.

Off screen, too, something of the characters she plays on screen can be detected, and countless anecdotes only reinforce the impression we are left with on seeing Marlene's films. One of the most striking traits of her

Marlene Dietrich.... Your name sounds at first like a
caress and becomes the crack of a whip. You
wrap yourself in feathers and furs which seem
to belong to your body like fur to a wolf
or feathers to an ostrich. Your voice, your gaze
is like the Lorelei's, but the Lorelei was
dangerous; you are not, because the secret
of your eternal beauty lies in never losing sight of your heart.
JEAN COCTEAU

character is, for example, her sense of humour. Right from the start of her career in the U.S.A. she has played the Hollywood game with apparent effortlessness and her tongue firmly in her cheek. The first woman to wear trousers, she justified herself by saying it was simply more comfortable. She used to turn up at Hollywood parties wearing a tuxedo, always accompanied by a new admirer, often hand-picked from a range of the biggest stars of the day. In about 1940 she started talking about what she fancied might happen at her funeral. Rudolph Sieber, her husband, would be at the entrance of the church, checking out the guests and throwing out the imposters; Jean Gabin would be leaning against the doorway, in a black mood, a cigarette drooping from his lips; Gary Cooper would be yawning, and James Stewart frantically trying to find out who was being buried; Douglas Fairbanks Jr would be in his naval uniform, while Erich Maria Remarque would get the church wrong and go to another funeral.

Her spontaneous nature shines through as much in her private life as in her films. In 1954, when she had been appearing at the Café de Paris in London, she went to sing in a home for blind children, then to the hospital bed of a man with terminal cancer who longed to meet her. While making *Café Electric* in 1927 the producer, who had instantly fallen in love with her, became seriously ill and knew he would not recover. He had a single wish: to see Marlene's legs one last time. Unhesitatingly she complied.

From her childhood Marlene had had a habit of developing sudden infatuations for people. At seventeen it was the actress Henny Porten: Marlene saw all her films and avidly collected photographs of her; she spent hours watching out for her, sometimes even playing the violin at her window. But the first time Henny Porten invited her to dinner Marlene was completely tongue-tied.

These demonstrations of affection often take unexpected forms. It is very important for Marlene to play a part in the domestic life of those she cares for. She once suggested to the socialist writer Mercedes d'Acosta, the day after meeting her at a Hollywood party in the 1930s, that she should come and cook for her. When success brought her into contact with Alexander Fleming, the discoverer of penicillin – the antibiotic which had saved her own life several years previously – Marlene invited him round for a meal cooked by herself.

Of course, her family were the first to benefit from this particular facet of her personality. When her daughter moved to New York with her husband in 1947, Marlene, clad in trousers and with a scarf tied round her head, started scrubbing the walls and floors, with the result that she fooled the neighbours into thinking that she was the charlady. On another occasion, out walking with her grandchildren, she dressed up as a nanny. Greta Garbo, noticing two lovely children being looked after by a very elegant nanny, stopped to admire the babies and, looking up, recognized Dietrich. As far as these last two stories go, Marlene stoutly denies in her memoirs (*Nehmt nur mein Leben*) ever having deliberately gone incognito. So we will have to take these anecdotes at face value – bearing in mind, however, that in her memoirs she tends not to wear her heart entirely on her sleeve.

Friendship is also very important to Marlene, and she has always shown immense loyalty to her friends. In the mid-1930s John Gilbert had been deserted by Garbo, and his career was in ruins because his unfortunately high-pitched voice did not suit talkies. Gradually he was becoming an alcoholic, so Marlene took him in hand and tried to procure him the lead in the film she was about to make, *Desire* (1935). One day, when they had both been by the swimming pool, Garbo came to the door and Gilbert stood for an hour on the doorstep talking to her. Marlene went home immediately. Left alone once more, Gilbert started drinking again, and died soon after. By way of atonement for what she believed to be her fault, Marlene took Gilbert's daughter under her wing for many years.

When France was liberated, she used her influence to defend Maurice Chevalier, who had sung for the Germans. In 1947 enraptured by his performance in *Caligula* at the Théâtre Hébertot, she very actively tried to find a part for Gérard Philipe on her return to

Opposite and above: Morocco, 1930. Amy Jolly (Marlene Dietrich) receiving legionnaire Tom Brown (Gary Cooper) in her bedroom, the scene referred to on page 10; an extract from the screenplay is on page 38. From the first picture to the third her facial expression changes from weariness to nonchalant irony

This page
Above, top and bottom: With Carole
Lombard, Lily Damita and Errol
Flynn at a party given by Carole
Lombard in the amusement park in
Venice, California, on 21 June
1935
Right, above: Paying Charlie
Chaplin a visit on the set of City
Lights, 1931
Right, below: With Groucho Marx
in the 1930s
Opposite
Left, above: With Rouben
Mamoulian, Jean Harlow and Josef
von Sternberg in the 1930s

Left, centre: With Katharine Hepburn
and Douglas Fairbanks Jr at a party
in the 1930s
Left, below: With Dorothy Arzner,
Josef von Sternberg and Wallace Beery
on the set of von Sternberg's Sergeant
Madden
Right, above: With Maurice
Chevalier and Gary Cooper in
Hollywood in 1932, attending the
première of Cecil B. de Mille's The
Sign of the Cross
Right, below: With John Kobal and
Mischa Spoliansky (right) in London,
1965. Spoliansky composed some of
her 1920s' Berlin songs

Hollywood. And in the 1950s, having been a bridesmaid at the ill-fated wedding of Edith Piaf and Jacques Pills, Marlene did her best to help Edith get over it.

Her loyalty and generosity combine at times with an unexpected sense of decency and impulsiveness, as demonstrated in this last anecdote. Mercedes McCambridge, one of her best friends, rang one day from Los Angeles with the news that her baby had died. Marlene, who was in New York, hung up quickly, and Mercedes McCambridge was dismayed. Less than twenty-four hours later, Marlene arrived on her doorstep.

HER HUSBAND

Anyone who is interested in the cinema has some idea of the life and films of Marlene Dietrich. Who doesn't know that a film director discovered her and started her on her career in a film called *The Blue Angel*, that she became a star, that she sang for the Allied soldiers during the Second World War, and that finally she began a new career in show business? However, few people know that Marlene Dietrich married at twenty-three and never divorced. Gossip columnists have regularly reminded us of the existence of her husband, but in general Marlene, who has always been very discreet about her love life, has managed to maintain a high degree of privacy.

On 17 May 1924 Marlene married Rudolph Sieber, an assistant producer who had helped her obtain various parts. He was handsome and, as she says in her memoirs, 'well brought up', and Marlene wanted to have a child.

After the birth of Heidede (who later became Maria), Marlene spent some time at home looking after her. But shortage of work meant that Rudi found it hard to keep the household solvent, and Marlene went back to the theatre and cinema. Very soon she also regained her personal independence, and to begin with Rudi suffered greatly. But in 1927 he struck up a relationship with a friend of Marlene's, a Russian actress called Tamara Matul, by whose side he stayed until her death in 1968.

This page: About the time of The Devil is a Woman, *1935*
Opposite: About the time of Desire, *1935*

16

About the time of The Garden
of Allah, *1936*

This was the start of a long, firm friendship – though it seems odd to speak of friendship between husband and wife. Rudi and Tamara lived at first in Paris, then left Europe during the war and settled in New York. Rudi worked as an assistant producer in cinema and radio, often thanks to Marlene (he was, for example, von Sternberg's assistant on *The Devil is a Woman* in 1935). The couple would frequently stay with Marlene and Maria.

The latter part of Rudi's life was not very happy and for Marlene, who went on seeing him regularly, it was a constant source of sorrow. In 1953 Rudi, out of work and depressed, had to undergo major surgery for a stomach ulcer. He recovered, though barely, and was considerably weakened and incapable of continuing to work on a regular basis. He retired to a ranch in the San Fernando valley at Sylmar, not far from Los Angeles, where he lived with Tamara, entirely cut off from the world and cared for by a German nurse, Eva Wiere, who looked after him until he died. Rudi and Tamara regularly had Marlene to stay, plus a few faithful friends such as Hans Kohn and his wife. But the atmosphere at the ranch was gloomy. Mercedes McCambridge tells how, each time Marlene returned from one of these visits, she would be in tears.

In the early 1960s Rudi suffered another setback when Tamara, who was a very unstable person, went into a rest home at Camarillo near Los Angeles. Rudi was distraught. As during other crises, Marlene was often at his side – she gave him support again after the earthquake at Sylmar in 1971. Rudi had promised Marlene never to give interviews or refer to their marriage. He only granted one interview – to the *Herald Tribune* – but he disclosed virtually nothing about Marlene, as she herself about him. Rudi died in June 1976, but Marlene was unable to attend his funeral.

It is very difficult to know what to make of this rather odd marriage which, nevertheless, constitutes part of Dietrich's personality. Why did she never obtain a divorce? Perhaps to benefit from the protection it gave her when it came to other men? And how close did she come to divorce when she met men like Remarque or Gabin?

In her memoirs Marlene presents Rudi as a friend in whom she had total trust and for whom she felt great affection. This marriage might be seen as a test of fidelity. As Hemingway once said, 'Marlene has laid down her own rules in her life, but the norms of behaviour and the rules of decorum that she imposes on herself are no less rigid than the Ten Commandments.'

Their days in Germany, their shared experiences as expatriates and, of course, their daughter, forged intimate bonds. Marlene always consulted Rudi when it came to making important decisions. Originally a husband, his role changed to that of an older brother. That, too, is typically feminine: a woman who ceases to love often tries to keep her lover as a friend. And with Marlene the lack of a real brother could only have reinforced this feeling. We could go on for ever trying to analyze this relationship, but the most important thing, in order to understand as much as possible of Marlene Dietrich as a person, is to know that it existed.

In London, about the time of Stage Fright, *1950*

HER DAUGHTER

**My life today would be very empty were it not
for my daughter and my grandsons. Children
give you a reason to go on living.
There's always the possibility
they might need you. Without them you
might as well not exist.**

MARLENE DIETRICH

The relationship between Marlene and her daughter is more conventional than that between her and her husband. There have been difficult times – at the beginning of Marlene's career as a Hollywood star, for instance, and when Maria started having boyfriends. But the two women have always got back together again, and today Maria is, undoubtedly, Marlene's only true support.

When Heidede (Maria) was a year old and Marlene started working again, Rudi looked after her. In the early 1930s Marlene, setting out for the U.S.A. for the first time, left her daughter behind in Germany. When she came back at the end of the year, she found little Heidede was ill. So she stayed five months in Germany and nursed her devotedly until April 1931, when she took her with her to America.

The two of them went to live in a beautiful rented house in Beverly Hills and it was at this stage that Heidede assumed the name of Maria. It was also about now that Marlene's life became extremely eventful – never a day passed without her being in the news. One day she received a threat that Maria was to be kidnapped, and as a result she sentenced her daughter to near total solitary confinement: Maria received her education from tutors at home, and she only went out in the company of chauffeurs and bodyguards. In 1933, aged eight, Maria played Marlene as a child in *The Scarlet Empress*. She was stunningly beautiful then, but very quickly started to show the strain of the way of life imposed on her by her mother – both sheltered and dissolute – and she started to put on weight.

In 1936 Marlene took Maria to London. Then, although she did visit her daughter regularly, she went off on her own, leaving Maria in a boarding school in Switzerland. In 1937 Marlene, Rudi, Maria and Tamara spent a holiday together on the Riviera.

On her return to Los Angeles, Maria decided to become an actress. She took lessons from the famous director Max Reinhardt who, in order to escape the Nazis, had settled in New York. Maria appeared in several plays and was acclaimed by the critics, and about this time she fell in love with a producer called Dean Goodman. Having done some research on him, Marlene did her utmost to prevent the marriage, but it took place without her in Hollywood. Marlene refused ever to set eyes on Goodman, but still helped Maria whenever necessary.

Two years later Maria divorced and settled in New York, where she continued to work as an actress. Marlene was often in the audience, and sometimes even acted as her adviser. Maria played regularly on Broadway, went on the radio with Orson Welles, and taught drama at Fordham University.

She then met William Riva, a stage designer. They married quickly and, although this time Marlene did give the marriage her seal of approval, she remained discreetly silent. To begin with, the young couple lived in a very modest apartment; a year later John Michael was born, making Marlene in 1948 a stunningly beautiful grandmother. At that juncture Marlene insisted that they moved, and bought them a house: she helped them to move in, among other things unloading a furniture van and, as usual, conducting a thorough spring-clean.

In the early 1950s Marlene was still offering help and support to Maria in both her professional and domestic life. But in 1958 Maria, by now a mother of four, decided to give up the stage. She underwent a total transformation – she relaxed, blossomed, and became more like her mother every day. The Riva family went to stay in Rome for a while in the 1960s. As the years went by, Maria and her mother grew closer together. In 1973 Peter Riva, the second grandson, got married at the age of twenty-two. Marlene couldn't get to the wedding, but the next thing she knew she was a great-grandmother. When Marlene broke her leg twice in the mid-1970s, Maria was at her side, and she was with her, too, for the making of *Just a Gigolo* in 1978, the last film in which Marlene appeared.

Today Maria and her children have become, without

a shadow of a doubt, Marlene's only reason to go on living. The moment she runs into a problem she knows she can rely on Maria, and in her memoirs she shows genuine admiration for Maria as a mother.

HER MOTHER AND SISTER

Marlene has been so reticent about her forebears that it is difficult to be precise. Her mother, Wilhelmina Elisabeth Josephine Felsting, whose family were jewellers, married Louis Erich Dietrich in 1883 when she was seventeen. Dietrich had been a major in the Uhlan cavalry regiment and had served courageously during the Franco-Prussian war, for which he was awarded the Iron Cross. He then became an officer in the German police force, a highly esteemed post in those days.

Marlene's mother was very beautiful. She had been strictly brought up, an attitude she applied to her own children while nevertheless showing great affection to them. Marlene's older sister, Elisabeth, was born in 1900, and Marlene herself a year later. In 1911 their father died and Frau Dietrich had to go out to work in order to support her children. Fairly soon she married another soldier, Colonel Edward von Losch, who died at the end of the First World War. So, as a child, Marlene had to endure first the sudden death of her father when she was only about ten, and then the total absence of men, something she alludes to often in her memoirs.

Her mother did not relish the prospect of her daughter going into the theatre. However, she never stopped giving her her full support and approved of her marriage to Rudolph Sieber. At the end of 1930 she met Marlene in London for the première of *Morocco*, a film she didn't much care for, and they went back together to Berlin.

After Hitler came to power in 1933 Marlene, not wishing to return to Berlin, met her mother in Switzerland. She tried, unsuccessfully, to persuade her mother and sister to leave Germany. Once war had broken out she heard no word from them until 1945. Throughout the war Marlene was extremely worried about what might happen to them, especially when she went on tour singing to the Allies. However, in her capacity as the widow of an officer from the front line (her second husband), Marlene's mother was not pestered. On the other hand Elisabeth, who had become a schoolteacher, was not so lucky. Goebbels, who was furious with Marlene for the way she was behaving, had Elisabeth thrown into the concentration camp at Belsen – where, all the same, she did get preferential treatment. Marlene personally went to find her again when the camp was liberated.

In September 1945 Marlene went to see her mother in Berlin, and they spent several days together. But Marlene had to leave for Biarritz to see a retrospective view of her work which had been organized for the army. When she arrived she received a telephone call announcing her mother's sudden death.

In the 1960s Elisabeth retired. Marlene supported her financially, and occasionally went to see her. She died in Berlin in 1974.

If her mother and sister seem to constitute the whole of her childhood and adolescence, we have to bear in mind that, from the early 1930s onwards, Marlene had

Opposite
Above: With her daughter Maria in 1931.
Below: Marlene and Maria at the première of Judy Garland's show at the Palace, 17 October 1951

This page
Above: With Maria and Rudolph Sieber in the 1930s
Below: Reunion with her mother at Berlin Airport, 19 September 1945

severed virtually all her connections with Germany. She was still fond of the country, but the fact that she had experienced war from the other side put a strain on her relationship with her homeland and, in particular, put a strain on the only real ties there that were left to her: her mother and her sister.

HER MEN

Besides, everything's much simpler than that. There are no Ten Commandments when it comes to love; there is only one: to love unconditionally.
MARLENE DIETRICH

Apart from Rudolph Sieber, her husband, Josef von Sternberg, her director, and, in later days, Burt Bacharach, her band leader, it appears that two men, as different as chalk from cheese, have made a major

impression on her life: the writer Erich Maria Remarque and the actor Jean Gabin. The way she talks about them in her memoirs would seem to confirm this.

As for Ernest Hemingway, he and Marlene shared mutual admiration and enormous affection, as can be seen from what he wrote about her (see page 152), but it seems that they were never more than just very good friends. It is more interesting to concentrate on the two relationships mentioned above, for Remarque's intellectualism and Gabin's practical intelligence reflect, yet again, the two sides of Marlene's character.

Erich Maria Remarque Their paths crossed for the first time in Berlin in 1928. Remarque was not yet famous and Marlene's name was at that time often associated with Willi Forst, opposite whom she played in *Café Electric* and who later became a great director. But it was in Venice in the mid-1930s that, when von Sternberg introduced them to each other, they felt a mutual affinity.

Remarque had fought in the First World War and lived in Switzerland on Lake Maggiore in a lovely house embellished by superb paintings – his particular passion was the Impressionists. He had been married, divorced, then remarried, and was world-famous at the time for his novel *All Quiet on the Western Front*. Unable to cope with his own company, he was subject to bouts of deep depression and drank far too much. Marlene was intrigued by both his intelligence and his reputation for living on his wits. They spent a lot of time together between 1937 and 1943 – on holiday at the Hôtel du Cap on the Riviera, in Paris, in New York, and in Hollywood which, however, Remarque loathed. In about 1943 they started drifting apart, though they were still very involved with each other. Dietrich would very much have liked the part of Joan Madou in *Arch of Triumph*, a character for which she herself may have provided the inspiration to Remarque. The film was made in 1945 with Ingrid Bergman.

In 1957 their marriage was rumoured in the press, but Remarque married Paulette Goddard and moved permanently to Switzerland. They hardly saw each other again, something which constantly saddened Marlene.

Marlene Dietrich does, of course, speak of Remarque a good deal in her memoirs. His talent, his refinement, and his erudition enabled Marlene to satisfy her thirst for art and literature. But she also highlights his pessimism and his tendency to lapse into melancholy. Perhaps Marlene was too much in love with life to tolerate this negative streak in his personality. Nevertheless, it does

Opposite: With Erich Maria Remarque in New York, 1939
Left: With Jean Gabin at El Morocco in New York after the première of Gabin's first Hollywood film, Moontide, 1942. Archie Mayo directed, replacing Fritz Lang

seem that she seriously considered getting divorced in order to marry Remarque.

Jean Gabin Marlene's relationship with Jean Gabin lasted nowhere near as long as the one with Remarque. Perhaps they were drawn to each other because they lived through and experienced the war in the same fashion. Gabin's masculinity and strength of personality fascinated Marlene. It is interesting to note that she speaks of him in her memoirs as a very sensitive and very fragile man – someone whom she felt able to protect.

She met Gabin for the first time when on holiday on the Riviera with Remarque. There was a possibility of her appearing with him and Jules Raimu in *Dédé d'Anvers*, but never-ending arguments about the screenplay caused the project to be abandoned.

They met again in 1941 when Gabin arrived in Hollywood to work under contract for Darryl F. Zanuck. By now Marlene had him at her beck and call. They moved into a small house rented from Greta Garbo and socialized with the rest of the French community, including Marcel Dalio, and Jean Renoir and his wife. Gabin, however, did not like Hollywood and felt rather guilty doing nothing but basking in the sun.

In 1943 he left to join the Allied Forces in North Africa,

but they continued to write to each other. Marlene tells how on one of her tours she bumped into him on the road. She waved and shouted: he turned round, looked at her in astonishment, cried '*Merde!*' and vanished . . . .

After the Liberation, they were inseparable for nearly two years. At first they worked together on Marcel Carné's film *Les Portes de la Nuit* (*Gates of the Night*), but Marlene's unreasonable demands drove Carné to exasperation and both dropped the project. Another film, *Martin Roumagnac*, did materialize: it was an unmitigated disaster. Gabin became extremely jealous and they argued constantly. Marlene talks of how he would like to have married her and had a child together.

Marlene went back to Hollywood, Gabin married soon after, and they never saw each other again. Jean Marais remembers how in the 1950s Dietrich often asked him to go and sit with her in a café opposite the apartment block where Gabin lived. She would also ask him to go with her to see Gabin's films.

One can see why Marlene was so taken by this man, despite their very different temperaments. She was attracted to his very strong personality, combined with tremendous sensitivity and irreproachable uprightness of character. *Martin Roumagnac*, in other respects not a very good film, is very indicative of their relationship.

DIETRICH'S LIFE AND CAREER

Germany

Everything there is to say about me has been said.
I'm nothing special, nothing spectacular.
A director said to me one day ' Come on, let's have Marlene.'
'Who is this Marlene?' I asked him. I don't know....

MARLENE DIETRICH

arlene Dietrich was born Maria Magdalene Dietrich in Berlin, at 54 Kaiserallee in the Schöneberg district, on 27 December 1901. The date of her birth, a subject of debate for some time, has been confirmed by authorities at the East German Archives and by Marlene's own celebration of her eightieth birthday in 1981.

At the age of five, Maria Magdalene went to the Auguste Victoria School, a highly disciplined institution where she received an excellent education. A shy, studious girl, she learned French at an early age (thanks partly to a French governess) and became an avid reader. Heine, Dostoievsky, Erich Kästner and especially Goethe were among her favourite writers. She also became fascinated with the theatre, admiring in particular the great actress Eleanora Duse, and excelled at both the piano and the violin. Throughout her childhood she always tried to appear older than she really was.

Maria left school in 1918 and in the following year went to study at the Weimar conservatoire of music. Her mother would have liked her to pursue a career in music, but a health problem forced her to abandon this idea. It was at this point that Maria decided, against her mother's wishes, to become an actress. With this aim in mind she moved to Berlin.

The atmosphere in Berlin was bleak in those days: cynicism and immoderation

In a Berlin revue called Broadway, 1927. *Marlene is the first dancer on the left*

Above: His Greatest Bluff,
*1927. Yvette (Marlene
Dietrich) and Henry Devall
(Harry Piel)*
Left: Three Loves, *1929.
Stascha (Marlene Dietrich)
and Henry Leblanc (Uno
Henning)*

abounded, and it was difficult for an aspiring young actress to make a living. Maria filled her time taking English lessons, and made a little money selling gloves on commision and playing the violin to accompany silent movies. Her only theatrical appearances were as a singer and dancer in third-rate cabarets and musical reviews such as those staged by Guido Theilder and Rudolph Nelson. It was at this time that Maria changed her name to Marlene (MARia MagdaLENE).

Despite her limited success, Marlene remained devoted to the theatre. In 1921 she auditioned for the school run by Max Reinhardt, the most fashionable theatre director of the time. She did not get a place, but one of Reinhardt's assistants, Berthold Held, took her on and, after a year's training, she started to get small parts in plays produced at Reinhardt's theatres.

Marlene's film career began in 1922 with *The Little Napoleon* (*Der kleine Napoleon*), directed by Georg Jacoby and starring Egon von Hagen, Paul Heidemann and Harry Liedtke. She had a minor part as a maid.

The same year she appeared in *Tragedy of Love* (*Tragödie der Liebe*), directed by Joe May, with Erika Glassner, Mia May and Emil Jannings, whom she met again six years later in *The Blue Angel*. Rudolph Sieber was Joe May's assistant and it seems that he was instrumental in getting her the part.

In 1923 she appeared in another film, *Man by the Roadside* (*Der Mensch am Wege*), a film produced and directed by Wilhelm (later William) Dieterle, whom she came across again in Hollywood when he was a prestigious director – he would direct Marlene in

The Blue Angel, 1929. Lola Lola (Marlene Dietrich) and Mazeppa (Hans Albers)

Kismet in 1944. In 1924 in *Leap into Life* (*Der Sprung ins Leben*) she played a young ingenue alongside Paul Heidemann. During this period she continued acting on the stage, taking minor parts in plays by Shakespeare, Somerset Maugham, Wedekind and Sternheim.

Soon after this Marlene took a break from acting and devoted two years to her family. In 1924 she had married Rudolph Sieber, and soon she was the mother of a baby daughter. This was a happy time for her. When she took up films again, encouraged by Sieber himself, she realized that she would have to start from the beginning again. Her first job was as an extra in *The Joyless Street*, released in the U.S. as *The Street of Sorrow* (*Die freudlose Gasse*), by G.W. Pabst. The star of the film, Greta Garbo, left shortly afterwards for Hollywood. Marlene next landed a slightly bigger part as Micheline in *Manon Lescaut*, directed by Arthur Robinson with Lya de Putti as Manon. A modest success in Germany, it was the first of Marlene's films to cross the Atlantic.

Then in 1926 Marlene made two films by Alexander Korda, *A Modern Du Barry* (*Eine Du Barry von Heute*) and *Madame Wants No Children* (*Madame wünscht keine Kinder*). She appeared briefly in the latter and only accepted the part because Rudolph was Korda's assistant on the film. Later, in 1937, Korda asked Dietrich to come to London and appear in *Knight Without Armour*.

From 1926 onwards Marlene began to acquire a certain notoriety within Berlin's artistic circles. She was already wearing flamboyant clothes, was not afraid of showing off her legs, and had adopted a free and easy lifestyle.

When the play *Broadway*, a tremendous success in New York and London, transferred to Berlin, it was the dream of every young actress to appear in it. Marlene landed only a small part, but the play was received with wild enthusiasm by both the public and the critics, and Marlene achieved some prominence.

Marlene then made two films for Ellen Richter Films, a German company. Directed by Willi Wolff, these were *Heads Up, Charlie!* (*Kopf hoch, Charly!*) and *The Imaginary Baron* (*Der Juxbaron*). The star of both was Reinhold Schunzel, who later became a fine supporting actor in Hollywood, particularly in Hitchcock's *Notorious*. Another film Marlene appeared in at this time was *His Greatest Bluff* (*Sein grösster Bluff*), produced and directed by Harry Piel.

Marlene had become very friendly with Willi Forst, then an actor and later a director, while working in *Broadway*. During the play's run in Vienna, Forst virtually bulldozed

In a revue called Zwei Kravatten *(Two Neckties) with Hans Albers, 1929. As he watched the show, von Sternberg became convinced of Marlene's potential as an actress*

her into making a film there with him. This was *Café Electric*, the first film in which Marlene's legs were on full display. The film was produced by Count Sasha Kolvstat, whom Marlene would later visit when he was on his deathbed.

Returning to Berlin, Marlene found the atmosphere in the city somewhat depressing. But she continued performing in a range of cinema and theatre productions. Her singing in a 1928 revue called *It's in the Air* was well received, and so were her performances in two Bernard Shaw plays. She appeared in two films at this time, both produced by Robert Land *The Art of Love (Prinzessin Olala)* and *I Kiss Your Hand, Madame (Ich küsse ihre Hand, Madame)*. In this latter film she sang with Richard Tauber, whose voice was used for the leading part of Harry Liedtke. It is interesting to note that the assistant cameraman on this film was Fred Zinnemann, who was to go on to direct *High Noon* and *A Man For All Seasons*.

Marlene had already begun to stand out from other actresses on account of her eccentricities. She adored classical music and took a gramophone with her everywhere so that she could listen to Debussy, Ravel and Irving Berlin. Superstitious by nature, she would not be separated from her two dolls – a Japanese one and a golliwog. These lucky mascots even appear in *Morocco*, where they are Amy Jolly's constant companions.

Marlene now played her first *femme fatale* role in *Three Loves (Die Frau, nach der man sich sehnt)* by Kurt Berhardt (who became Curtis Bernhardt in Hollywood and directed Humphrey Bogart, Barbara Stanwyck and Bette Davis among others). The film was originally distributed as a silent in 1929 and had a soundtrack added in 1931. Her last silent film was a French-German co-production, *The Ship of Lost Men (Das Schiff der verlorenen Menschen)*, directed by Maurice Tourneur, assisted by his son, Jacques. Though visually beautiful, it was not a great commercial success.

In 1929 she appeared in her first talkie, *Dangers of the Engagement Period (Gefahren der Brautzeit)*, directed by Fred Sauer and starring Willi Forst. At the same time she was lined up to play Lulu in Pabst's *Pandora's Box*, but Pabst discovered Louise Brooks in *A Girl in Every Port* and Marlene was dropped.

The Ship of Lost Men, *1929. T.W. Cheyne, a young American doctor (Robin Irvine), Miss Ethel, an aviator (Marlene Dietrich), and Grischa, the cook (Vladimir Sokoloff)*

Dangers of the Engagement Period, *1929. McClure (Ernst Stahl-Nachbaur) and Evelyne (Marlene Dietrich)*

*With Maurice Tourneur on
the set of* The Ship of Lost
Men

The Blue Angel, *1929.* Four
pictures of Marlene as Lola
Lola

THE BLUE ANGEL

During 1929 Marlene had been singing and dancing in a revue called *Zwei Kravatten* (*Two Neckties*), a huge success in Berlin. Her reputation was by now established in Germany and elsewhere in Europe. The myth had not yet been born, but the public had already taken note of her charm, her ambiguity, her legs and her *femme fatale* quality.

At the beginning of 1929 Josef von Sternberg arrived in Berlin from America, invited by the U.F.A. (Germany's chief production company) and producer Erich Pommer, at Emil Jannings' instigation, to direct Jannings in a film based on Heinrich Mann's novel, *Professor Unrath*. After an outstanding career in Germany Jannings had left for Hollywood where, thanks to Sternberg, he had won an Oscar for his performance in *The Last Command* (1928).

Von Sternberg had caused a stir in 1925 with his first film, *The Salvation Hunters*, made on a shoestring. Charles Chaplin produced one of his films, *The Sea Gull*, with Edna Purviance, but it was never released. In 1928 he had made the first-ever gangster film, *Underworld*, with Clive Brook (with whom he worked again on *Shanghai Express* in 1932), Evelyn Brent and George Bancroft. He made several films with Bancroft, including the magnificent *The Docks of New York* (1928) and *Thunderbolt* (1929), his first talkie.

A flamboyant personality – impossibly so, according to some – he himself had added the aristocratic 'von' to his surname. Rather short and not very good-looking, but very shrewd and alert, he used to carry a cane, adopt poses, and spout witticisms. During the filming of *The Masked Bride* he is said to have been so dissatisfied with the actress he had had forced on to him, that he first pointed the camera at the ceiling, then stopped shooting altogether. He had a number of problems with his producers, which is one reason why he was not too prolific a film-maker and why several projects were dropped along the way.

On arriving in Berlin von Sternberg set about finding a leading lady for his new picture. He had wanted Brigitte Helm, but she was not available. Marlene Dietrich was first recommended by someone at the U.F.A., and they met one evening at dinner; but while he conceded that she had a very beautiful body, he was not so keen on her face. What was more, the producer Erich Pommer – who in any case had his own ideas, as did Jannings – was not at all enthusiastic.

Von Sternberg's attitude changed completely, however, when he went to see *Zwei Kravatten*, where he found Marlene singing. He immediately decided to audition her,

but Marlene was not really tempted. She hated the cinema, to start with, and was far from convinced that she had any talent at all. But despite the opposition of the producers and Jannings, and Marlene's own lack of enthusiasm, von Sternberg was adamant. The filming of *The Blue Angel* began on 4 November 1929.

Working conditions were tough: the German and English versions were shot on alternate days, and von Sternberg insisted on strict chronological order, which infuriated the producers. From the outset his relationship with Marlene was tense and highly charged. Every evening they would watch the rushes together. Marlene, fascinated, discussed them with him for hours and they never left each other's sides. At the start of the filming von Sternberg had cabled Paramount, asking them to put Marlene under contract. Adolph Zukor came out to Berlin, saw the rushes and offered her a contract on the spot.

The rest of the company were driven to distraction by von Sternberg's and Marlene's behaviour. Von Sternberg's wife, Merri, went back to the U.S.A. and Jannings, aware

As Lola Lola in The Blue Angel

The Blue Angel. *Immanuel Rath (Emil Jannings)*

that Marlene had superseded him as the star of the film, very nearly strangled her during one rehearsal. But von Sternberg continued to film.

As soon as the last day of filming was over, von Sternberg returned to the U.S.A. At each of its three previews *The Blue Angel* was stupendously received. On the evening of the third preview, Marlene herself boarded a ship for America. In three weeks she was to become famous throughout Europe, and in six months she would be a star across America.

Josef von Sternberg

When extreme emotions blend in the depths of a person,
when they burst out and when the entire mind
flows like lava from a volcano, the cold calculations of reason
have not presided over this emission, and who knows
where or when the work was started?

PAUL GAUGUIN

There are not only two sides to every story
but close to a thousand and the chances are that not
one of them is completely trustworthy.
One side of the story that concerns my relationship with Frau Dietrich
has long ago been told with the camera in seven films,
and it would not surprise me if it was the least trustworthy of all.

JOSEF VON STERNBERG

The interaction between director and actor is crucial to the success of a film. Some need perfect harmony, while others maintain a certain degree of tension, but the moment indifference strikes the relationship dies and it is all too obvious on the screen. What makes von Sternberg's films so fascinating, especially those starring Marlene Dietrich, is not just the sheer magical credibility of the image but the depth of feeling in Dietrich's performances: they imbue the simplest of story lines with an unforgettable pitch of intensity.

Undoubtedly von Sternberg was impossible to live with, and the atmosphere he created on a film set was unbearable. He was particularly unrelenting with Dietrich. Sometimes a scene had to be rehearsed a hundred times, and he frequently reduced her to tears, yet he never congratulated or encouraged her. Despite this, long after their last film Marlene, standing on the same set, is reputed to have picked up the microphone in a quiet moment and whispered, 'Where are you, Jo?'

Whenever von Sternberg refers to her in his autobiography his tone is bitter. But once they had stopped working together his appeal at the box office diminished. He did make two fine though only moderately successful films, *The Shanghai Gesture* and *The Saga of Anatahan*, but in both the spirit of Marlene Dietrich is curiously present.

The most common interpretation of their relationship is that he was wildly in love with her and frustrated to find he could not make her love him. But perhaps it is not that simple. The Gauguin quotation above was used by von Sternberg himself in the chapter on Marlene in his autobiography, and it says more than all the critics, psychologists and cinema historians put together. The spell which they cast over each other in the course of those five years and their seven films reached irrational, uncontrollable and inexplicable heights. The only way to try and grasp this strange relationship is to watch the films closely and study the evolution of Marlene's physical appearance and style of acting, and von Sternberg's style of filming.

Josef von Sternberg

Opposite: About the time of
Morocco, *1930*

*Above: With Merle Oberon
and Josef von Sternberg in
England, 1937, two years after
their separation. Von
Sternberg was in the process
of making* I Claudius, *which
was never completed, and
Dietrich* Knight Without
Armour

The Blue Angel was their first encounter, and as the film unfolds it reveals all the excitement of the initial discovery of the other person. Nothing has happened yet – nevertheless the die is cast. *Morocco* clearly conveys the stumbling-block in their relationship: lack of faith in the other. We feel that, in an atmosphere so tense you could cut it with a knife, they are nervously eyeing each other. Von Sternberg's camera pursues Marlene and scrutinizes her insistently. Her every movement seems all-important and critical, while the rhythm of the film is both slow and deliberate. The next four films (*Dishonored, Shanghai Express, Blonde Venus* and *The Scarlet Empress*) are coloured from one to the next by a distinct complacency, combined with a need to reach the point of confrontation and liberation. Marlene loses weight and grows more sophisticated, in the best sense of the word. Her style of acting is less ponderous, and stripped of unnecessary trappings; she dazzles us and becomes more provocative. She is swifter off the mark. Von Sternberg's style has in turn become faster, more exact, more sumptuous and more tense – notably with the introduction of incidental music. But the tension is now quite different; it is pitched higher, and literally explodes in *The Devil is a Woman* which symbolizes the dramatic zenith of their relationship and, by the same token, reflects the deadlock to which this relationship has brought them. Their romantic passage through these seven films is one of the most beautiful tales of the cinema.

When Marlene set off in 1939 from Germany on the *Bremen*, destined for America, she left Rudi and Heidede behind. She settled in Beverly Hills but, finding it difficult to adjust to the relaxed atmosphere of sun-drenched California, soon decided to return to Germany. Von Sternberg begged her to stay and began, a little too enthusiastically for the likes of his wife, Merri, to busy himself with Dietrich. The exasperated Merri even took Marlene to court later for alienation of affection. However, very quickly the shooting of *Morocco* began.

MOROCCO

Synopsis: Amy Jolly (Marlene Dietrich), a singer in a night club, arrives in Morocco by boat. On the ship she meets a wealthy dilettante, La Bessière (Adolphe Menjou), who promptly suggests he might be her patron. In the night club where she has just been offered a job, and where she is wildly successful, Amy also meets Tom Brown (Gary Cooper), a Foreign Legionnaire with a reputation for being something of a lady killer. A triangular situation develops; Amy and Tom are drawn to each other, then go their different ways, while La Bessière, resigned to his lot, just waits. When Tom is sent away on a mission, Amy, left on her own, agrees to marry La Bessière. But when the Legion returns without Tom, Amy, sick with worry, cannot stop herself going off to look for him, escorted by the unruffled La Bessière. Having found her legionnaire, she suddenly decides to follow him.

Amy: There's a Foreign Legion of women, too. But we have no uniforms – no flags – and no medals when we are brave.

Amy pulls at a medal which is pinned to the breast of Tom's tunic.

Amy: No wound stripes – when we are hurt.

Tom: Look here, is there anything I can do to help you?

Amy: No, I've heard that before. . . .

Close shot of Amy looking down sadly.

Amy: . . . or do you think you can restore my faith in men?

A portrait for Morocco,
1930

When von Sternberg left for America after shooting *The Blue Angel*, he took with him a small food hamper which Marlene had made up for him, and into which she had slipped a novel called *Amy Jolly*. This simple story of the love between a singer in a nightclub and a legionnaire became the basis for a screenplay written by von Sternberg, assisted by Jules Furthman, which he then offered to Paramount.

In poking fun at the story line and expressing himself more through images, von Sternberg quickly earned a reputation with the public and some critics as a decadent aesthete – a typical representative of the insouciance prevalent in 1930s' Hollywood. Perhaps, in *Morocco* and his next five films, von Sternberg did only aim to entertain the public and satisfy his own aesthetic and sentimental requirements. But an equally important aspect of his genius lies in what happened unconsciously: *Morocco* burst forth from him like lava from a volcano, and on the screen we see the real heart of the matter.

Morocco, 1930. La Bessière (Adolphe Menjou), Amy Jolly (Marlene Dietrich), Adjutant Caesar (Ulrich Haupt), and legionnaire Tom Brown (Gary Cooper)

The film deals with an abstract feeling, faith – faith in another, faith in one's self, faith in the future. The subject was touched on in *The Blue Angel*, but in *Morocco* it recurs in a more obvious, direct form: what prevents Tom and Amy being honest with each other is that they both lack faith – in themselves and in each other. When Marlene totters off on her high heels in pursuit of Tom's company of legionnaires in the desert, everyone laughs. The unreality of this ending is but the inevitable consequence of the story. How should the problem of the unreality of any passion be resolved? Sternberg's answer is clear: the only way out is faith in the unknown – a solution which, viewed from the outside, seems absurd.

Quite apart from its importance in the Sternberg–Dietrich story, *Morocco* is a very fine film. The dialogue is masterly and the use of the soundtrack very modern for 1930: the sequence where Marlene goes in search of Gary Cooper, who has supposedly been wounded, and finds him in a bar, is a classic of its kind. Von Sternberg uses the music of a pianist playing in the bar – whom however we cannot see – to heighten the scene's dramatic effect. Into this third-rate bar comes an elegant woman. The pianist keeps on playing the same tune, at a moderate tempo, breaking in the middle of an occasional line of dialogue, then resuming again. Films of that era which use sound so subtly are rare indeed.

There are many other equally clever scenes in *Morocco* – suffice it to say that, with *The Devil is a Woman*, *Morocco* is without doubt von Sternberg's most perfectly crafted film, and the one which best illustrates their relationship. Many people see the character played by Adolphe Menjou in *Morocco*, as well as that played by Lionel Atwill in *The Devil is a Woman*, as a reflection of von Sternberg himself. But it is never as easy to unravel the mystery of any work of art as it may at first appear. There is certainly a little of von Sternberg in Adolphe Menjou, and a little in Lionel Atwill (besides, their physical similarity is striking); but he is also Gary Cooper and Cesar Romero (in *The Devil is a Woman*) and even, at a pinch, Dietrich.

Von Sternberg and Dietrich give so much of themselves to these seven films that they polarize into a single personality. Thus they are able, aside from the plot and characters, to impart feelings with an intensity not often found in the cinema. It is this tight fusion of two people which gives these seven films their vitality.

With *Morocco* behind them, they immediately started on another film. Von Sternberg wanted to call it *X27*, but Paramount changed the title to *Dishonored*.

The closing image of Morocco. Imitating the woman camp followers, Amy Jolly, having thrown off her high heels walks into the desert after Tom Brown and his column of soldiers

Dishonored, *1931. As secret agent X27*
Opposite: X27 (Marlene Dietrich) and General Dymov (Wilfred Lucas) in Dishonored

Synopsis: The scene is set in Vienna during the First World War. The Head of the Secret Service (Gustav von Seyffertitz) employs a young prostitute (Marlene Dietrich), whom he meets by chance, to fulfil a dangerous assignment, having convinced himself of her loyalty and determination ('I'm not afraid of life or death!', she exclaims). She is given the code name X27. Having successfully completed this first assignment, X27 is despatched to unmask an agent from the Russian Secret Service who passes himself off as Lieutenant Kranau of the Austrian Army (Victor McLaglen).

After a series of adventures, with Kranau managing to elude X27, the bogus lieutenant is arrested on the Austrian border. X27 realises at this point that she has fallen in love with him. Left alone with him in his cell, she slips him her revolver and vanishes. She is duly accused of treason and sentenced to death by firing squad. The young lieutenant whose duty it is to carry out the sentence (Barry Norton), refuses to give the order to shoot because she is a woman. However another officer takes over and X27, having retouched her make-up, meets her death.

Von Sternberg uses this unlikely tale to show Dietrich in a number of surprising and provocative changes of costume. At the outset she is a cheap prostitute. Then, as necessitated by her work as a spy, she changes from a fur-trimmed long dress into a lamé mini-skirt; later she is transformed into a Russian peasant; finally she appears in trousers, boots and a leather jacket, and dies in a formal city outfit. It amounts to a kind of Dietrich festival, splendidly photographed by von Sternberg. Bridging the end of some scenes and the beginning of the next are long, breathtakingly beautiful, superimpositions. The story line pales into insignificance: what we are struck by is Dietrich's performance as an actress and von Sternberg's skill as a director.

Perhaps the most surprising scene in the film is the last. Employing a technique similar to that used in *Morocco*, von Sternberg makes this scene genuinely moving: by clever

Dishonored. *Four pictures of X27, disguised as a Russian peasant, as Colonel Kovrin (Lew Cody) pays court to her*

use of derision, irony and characterization he avoids the trap, which other people might have fallen into, of becoming over-melodramatic, though the circumstances seem so contrived that it is not immediately obvious what he is doing. When Marlene is sentenced to death, a young lieutenant, visibly very upset, goes with her to the death chamber. At the door of the chamber Marlene, looking calm and collected, asks him to draw his sword so that, in the reflection of its blade, she can retouch her make-up. When the soldier starts to cry, she uses the execution blindfold to wipe away his tears. The lieutenant refuses to give the execution order, and is replaced by an old officer, who does. The brutality of this ending contrasts with the intimacy and understanding between Marlene and the young lieutenant, and the effect of the film is thereby intensified.

Devices of this kind have caused von Sternberg to be the butt of much criticism. He has been accused of not being credible, of straying too far from reality in order to indulge his obsessions. Surely, though, the most important thing is that he draws us into the film and stirs our emotions.

Morocco, the first film von Sternberg and Dietrich made in the U.S.A. had already been a major success, both at the box office and in the eyes of the critics. With a huge publicity campaign behind her, Marlene was no longer an unfamiliar face. *The Blue Angel* and now *Dishonored*, which were released in the U.S.A. not long after *Morocco*, were also well received.

After making *Dishonored*, Marlene left to rejoin her daughter and husband, who had stayed behind in Germany. She was therefore present as *Morocco* was released in several European countries.

During this time, von Sternberg directed the only film he made without Marlene at this stage in his career, *An American Tragedy*, specially commissioned by Paramount. The film was to have been made by Eisenstein, but the studio rejected his screenplay and asked von Sternberg instead. The novel, by Theodore Dreiser, did not particularly inspire him, and it seems likely that the film would have been better had it been made at another time in von Sternberg's career.

Marlene returned to the U.S.A. in April 1931, this time accompanied by Maria (alias Heidede). Von Sternberg and Dietrich then embarked on their fourth film together.

X27 with Lieutenant Kranau (Victor McLaglen) on the Austrian border in a scene from Dishonored

Sentenced to death for high treason at the end of Dishonored, X27 emerges from her cell escorted by a priest and the young officer (Barry Norton) whose duty it is to carry out the sentence

About the time of Shanghai Express, *1932*

SHANGHAI EXPRESS

**'It took more than one man
to change my name to Shanghai Lily.'**

Synopsis: As the Shanghai Express prepares to leave the main railway station in Peking, the revolution in China is at its height. The first-class coach contains a mixed bag of individuals: an infamous adventuress called 'Shanghai Lily' (Marlene Dietrich), a bogus Eurasian merchant named Chang (Warner Oland), a young Chinese girl of dubious repute (Anna May Wong), a British medical officer (Clive Brook), an incorrigible gambler (Eugene Pallette), a boarding-house keeper (Louise Closser Hale), a disabled German peddling drugs (Gustav von Seyffertitz), a devout missionary (Lawrence

Shanghai recreated: Josef von
Sternberg on the set, 1932

Grant), and a retired French serviceman (Emile Chautard). The British medical officer recognizes Shanghai Lily as one of his past flames. Rebel soldiers attack the train and, in the course of interrogation supervised by the Eurasian merchant, who is in fact the leader of the rebels, we learn much about the background of these extraordinary personalities. Shanghai Lily resigns herself to becoming Chang's mistress in order to save the medical officer from being tortured by the rebels. But a sudden new development, which results in Chang's death, enables the passengers to reach Shanghai safely. Shanghai Lily and the medical officer are reunited.

Von Sternberg's style becomes progressively more concise and more studied. The plot is rather muddled, but China is recreated in the studio in an extraordinary way, while the supporting characters, though little more than vignettes, are very well drawn. But, over and above everything else, the photography is stunningly beautiful. In this, his fourth, and last film with von Sternberg, the director of photography, Lee Garmes, excelled himself. Some shots are almost like engravings, and of course, Marlene does particularly well out of this. She never looked more beautiful than in *Shanghai Express*.

On the set of Shanghai Express

This preoccupation with the aesthetic detracts to some extent from the film's emotional impact. Yet von Sternberg creates two or three quite astonishing scenes, as he often did. In one of them Shanghai Lily disappears into her carriage for a moment in near-darkness; then, in close-up, we see her slowly and hesitatingly joining her hands to pray for the medical officer, who is a prisoner of the rebels. It would doubtless be wrong to hunt too hard for hidden meanings in this digression. Von Sternberg, however, must surely have attached some importance to it, for the only person who catches Shanghai Lily in this pose is the devout missionary; as instructed by Marlene he breathes no word of it to anyone, but from that moment holds this 'creature' in high esteem, and is unable to refrain from mentioning the episode to the medical officer.

Shanghai Express itself was a great success, but other things were not going so well. It was the time of the kidnap threat to Maria, and Paramount attempted to cut von Sternberg out of their programme, finding him too extravagant. But Dietrich would not work with anyone else. All this friction contributed to the failure of their next film. Paramount could not make up their minds about the screenplay: von Sternberg was obliged to draw up a new story line, and in the end agreed reluctantly to begin the film. He then seemed quite deliberately to spend money wantonly, to spin things out and to become harder and harder to work with.

52

Blonde Venus, *1932. Helen Faraday (Marlene Dietrich) and her son Johnny (Dickie Moore)*
Left: At the opening of the film, happy with her young son
Opposite, above: Helen runs off with Johnny after her husband has started legal proceedings to assume custody of the child
Opposite, below: Finally, following her time in show business, they are reunited

BLONDE VENUS

Synopsis: Helen (Marlene Dietrich), a former night club singer of German nationality, lives happily in the U.S.A. with her husband, an American chemist (Herbert Marshall) and their son, Johnny (Dickie Moore). In order to save the life of her husband, a victim of potentially lethal radiation which cannot be treated except in Europe at vast expense, Helen decides to go back on the stage. She is an instant hit, and success brings her into contact with a young womanizer, Nick Townsend (Cary Grant), to whose charms she eventually succumbs. When he learns that Helen is working in order to pay for her husband's hospital treatment, Nick sets her up in one of his apartments. Her husband, now cured, returns from Europe and, bitterly upset by his wife's behaviour, starts legal proceedings to obtain custody of their son. Helen runs off with Johnny, and her husband has her followed by detectives. But Helen goes into hiding, often finding conditions very grim. When she is finally tracked down, Johnny is taken away from her. So she decides to further her career in show business, and becomes a celebrity in Parisian night club circles. Stopping over in New York, Nick Townsend urges her to see her husband and son. When he learns the reason why she went back on the stage, her husband forgives her and they are reconciled.

Blonde Venus is without doubt the least successful of the films made during the Dietrich–von Sternberg partnership. It casts little new light on the development of their working relationship, though it represents the first and last time that Marlene assumes the role of a mother on the screen. To be fair to the film, some scenes are interesting, some

sequences quite beautiful, some shots spectacular, and some musical interludes successful (notably the 'Hot Voodoo' number, where Marlene, removing her gorilla costume, emerges looking more beautiful than ever). But the lack of unity in the work as a whole, and particularly its tendency to border on the melodramatic, contributed greatly to its failure.

The public and the critics were growing weary of the von Sternberg–Dietrich duo. Von Sternberg took a trip to India; Marlene went off to New York, then to Paris, London and Berlin. It was then that Goebbels first asked her to remain in Germany. She declined and, on her return to Hollywood, Paramount still furious with von Sternberg, asked her to work with another director, Rouben Mamoulian whom von Sternberg recommended to her. The film was to be called *Song of Songs*.

Blonde Venus. *Marlene Dietrich as Helen Faraday. Opposite, above: Relaxing in her dressing-room just before she sings her famous number, 'Hot Voodoo' Opposite, below: With Nick Townsend (Cary Grant) Above: On stage in Paris*

*Song of Songs, 1933. Lily Czepanek (Marlene Dietrich), now Baroness von Merzbach, sees her former lover, Waldow (Brian Aherne), again
Opposite: On the set of* Song of Songs *with Rouben Mamoulian*

Falling in the middle of the von Sternberg series, this picture stands out on a limb. Rouben Mamoulian was very proud of it; in fact, this was the film that he showed to Greta Garbo to persuade her to play the title role in *Queen Christina*. Marlene plays a young peasant girl, just up from the country. She falls in love with an artist who comes to sculpt her in the nude. The artist's patron sees the statue, becomes enamoured with the subject, and marries Dietrich, who thus becomes a baroness. In the end, after many twists and turns in the plot, she is reunited with the sculptor.

With great skill and delicacy, Mamoulian manages to make this implausible story very nearly plausible. But if Dietrich seems to act more naturally than with von Sternberg (the critics commented that she seemed 'more human'), she is also more predictable. We feel that Mamoulian was not really at ease with Marlene, and that without von Sternberg at her side she is rather lost.

After making *Song of Songs* Marlene left to live for a while in Paris. There she found many other compatriots who had fled Germany after Hitler had come to power. From 1933 onwards she began to like Paris more and more, but she was not to have an apartment there until the Liberation. Meanwhile, von Sternberg was planning their sixth film, which was to be about Catherine the Great of Russia.

The Scarlet Empress, *1934.*
As the young German princess,
Sophia Frederica
Opposite: Playing with her
friends
Above: She has been requested
to present herself in the
drawing-room, as the
Empress's envoy has arrived
Below: Kissing the hand of
each member of the family
while her father, Prince August
(C. Aubrey Smith), looks on
sternly

THE SCARLET EMPRESS

Synopsis: A German princess, Sophia Frederica (played by both Maria Sieber and Marlene Dietrich, at different ages), shows signs from her earliest days of being destined for great things. The Empress of Russia (Louise Dresser) sends Count Alexis (John Lodge) to fetch her in order to marry her to the Grand Duke Peter (Sam Jaffe), the heir to the throne. On her arrival in St Petersburg, Sophia Frederica is renamed Catherine. She is dismayed to find that the Grand Duke Peter is a degenerate who shows a marked preference for his common-law wife, Countess Elizabeth (Ruthelma Stevens). Horrified by the goings-on at court, disappointed by her initial experiences and feeling

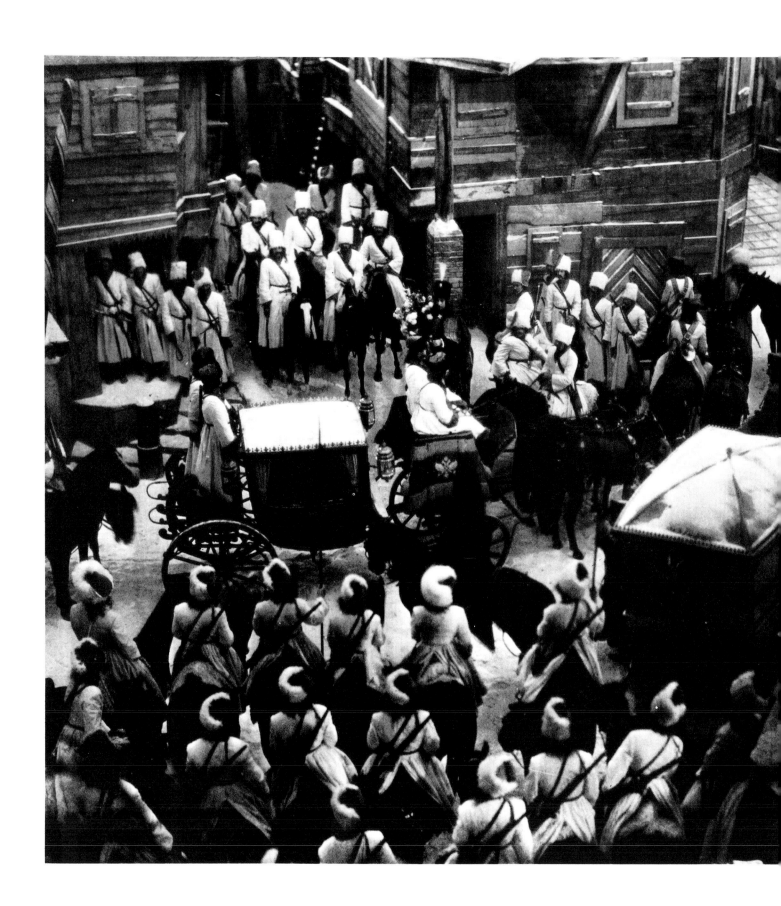

The Scarlet Empress. *On the long journey which will take the young German princess to St Petersburg*

neglected, Catherine begins to take lovers and go her own way. The Empress dies and the Grand Duke conspires to have Catherine assassinated. But she has the support of the army and many other followers, ranging from lovers and clergymen to discontented peasants. The Emperor is assassinated instead and Catherine is declared Empress of all the Russias.

It is a magnificent, extravagantly produced film, pulsating with energy as if von Sternberg had suddenly been released from constricting shackles. His style had become less static in *Blonde Venus*, but with this film, using a combination of the camera, careful editing and his famous superimpositions, von Sternberg transports us in just a few seconds to the very heart of Russia, and with that introduces a lavishness quite lacking in moderation. The artistic director, Hans Dreier, performs miracles in recreating the magic of the palace, though no doubt it is a mere figment of his imagination. In fact, we find rather that this extravaganza tends to swamp the actors themselves.

Nevertheless, Dietrich never ceases to surprise and look ravishingly beautiful as she changes from naïve girl to ambitious *femme fatale*. John Lodge, one of the few who was always prepared to stand up for von Sternberg right to the bitter end, gives a very polished performance. This is the film where Maria, aged eight, plays the role of her mother as a child with considerable charm.

The Scarlet Empress was a disaster at the box office. This can partly be attributed to the release a few months earlier of a film produced by Alexander Korda, entitled *Catherine of Russia*. Starring Elisabeth Bergner and Douglas Fairbanks Jr, the film was more moderate in tone and considered to be in better taste.

The Scarlet Empress. *On
the Empress's orders Sophia
Frederica is put in the hands
of the Court wigmakers and
dressmakers*

On top of this, the critics were scathing about von Sternberg's lavish extravaganza: they accused the film of being a piece of sheer folly, pretentious and ridiculous. Seeing it again today, we still come away dazzled by the ostentation of the direction. The future of von Sternberg's and Dietrich's collaboration was questioned at the time. The final decision really lay with him, for Dietrich was always fascinated by what he achieved with her on screen. For that reason, she tolerated his sudden changes of mood and begged him to continue working with her.

So von Sternberg set to work on the screenplay of what he was calling, even at the time, their last film. He drew his inspiration from a novel by Pierre Louÿs, *La Femme*

The Scarlet Empress.
*Neglected, and with her
illusions shattered, Catherine
embarks on a series of love
affairs
Opposite: With the Captain
of the Imperial Guard
Right, above: On the set just
before shooting the banquet
scene
Below: Playing blind man's
buff*

et le Pantin (The Woman and the Puppet). John Dos Passos was commissioned to help him write the screenplay, but he was ill for most of the time and von Sternberg worked virtually on his own. Von Sternberg wanted to call the film *Caprice Espagnol*, but Ernst Lubitsch, then Production Manager at Paramount, changed the title to *The Devil is a Woman*, and they finally agreed on this. In the violence of its emotion *The Scarlet Empress* had foreshadowed *The Devil is a Woman*, but in the new film von Sternberg was to be more in control of that violence.

*Following pages: After the
assassination of the Grand
Duke Peter, who had become
Emperor on his mother's death,
Catherine, thanks to support
from the army, is proclaimed
Empress of all the Russias*

*The Devil is a Woman,
1935. As Concha Perez
Opposite: At the carnival in
Seville
Above: In a night club in
Cadiz*

Synopsis: In 1890, while carnival is in full swing in Seville, Antonio Galvan (Cesar Romero), a young political refugee, makes the acquaintance of the infamous Concha Perez (Marlene Dietrich), with whom he arranges a rendezvous. Meanwhile, the young man meets a friend, Don Pasqual (Lionel Atwill), a former civil guard, who is one of the notorious lady's cast-offs. He describes how he was humiliated by Concha Perez and tries to dissuade Antonio from seeing her again. Listening to Don Pasqual's story only makes Antonio burn with desire for Concha, but, out of respect for his friend, he declares he will never set eyes on her again. However, he keeps their date. Don Pasqual then challenges Antonio to a duel and, convinced that Concha really loves Antonio, shoots into the air. Concha rushes to the bedside of the wounded Don Pasqual, but he orders her to leave. She goes off to Paris with Antonio. But no sooner has Antonio crossed the border than she returns to Don Pasqual's side.

First of all, it must be said that this is both von Sternberg's and Dietrich's favourite film. This time von Sternberg takes us to Spain, and the photography is quite breathtakingly beautiful. The film revolves around Dietrich, more ravishing than ever, brimming with

Right: Portrait for The Devil is a Woman

The Devil is a Woman
Opposite, above: Concha Perez and Antonio Galvan (Cesar Romero)
Opposite, below: Concha Perez and Don Pasqual (Lionel Atwill)

vitality and exuding nonchalance. Underlying the story of the mysterious *femme fatale* who causes trouble, then disappears, and the man who allows himself to be treated like dirt virtually to his dying day, we are left feeling that there is something we cannot put our finger on. Von Sternberg's aim is no longer as obvious as it was in *Morocco*, yet the basic ingredients are the same.

As in *Morocco* and *Dishonored*, it is in the ending of the film that von Sternberg has hidden the surprise. The *dénouement* is always crucial. Often it throws new light on the whole of the film, especially if it is contrary to what we were led to expect. Concha Perez had duped Don Pasqual all along, but when he is wounded she dashes impulsively to his bedside. He orders her to go and join his rival. She leaves with Antonio but deserts him suddenly and comes back, dressed in black from head to toe, to keep vigil over Don Pasqual's bedside.

Von Sternberg was once again accused of being a romantic; it was said that the black dress symbolized death. In fact the explanation is probably much simpler: this ending only assumes significance in relation to the rest of the film. It is this return, this sudden change of heart on the part of the character, this brief glimmer of hope which suddenly illuminate a film which is otherwise empty of hope. (Compare, for example, Pasolini's closing images in *Salo: The 120 Days of Sodom* or Jean Eustache's in *The Mother and the Whore*.) The whole film would seem geared to reach another conclusion: the *femme fatale*, weak men, the woman who kills the man, and so on. She ought to have left with her new lover, the implication being that she would, in due course, leave him for the next one.... Once again, von Sternberg found himself swimming against the tide.

The film had its share of problems when released. The critics virtually ignored it and

On the set of The Devil is a Woman

the Spanish Government took exception to the characterization of the civil guard, which they found insulting to their country. Not only was the screening of the film stopped, but the U.S. Department of State, not wishing to fuel international tension, asked Paramount to burn the negative. While they may not actually have done this, it is a fact that there are not many prints of the film in circulation today and, as might be expected, very few indeed in Europe.

Von Sternberg and Dietrich went their separate ways rather dramatically at the end of this film, announcing that they would never work together again. Once again the making of the film had been fraught with difficulties.

The conclusion of *The Devil is a Woman* can be seen as foreshadowing the conclusion of the von Sternberg–Dietrich story: von Sternberg is the injured party, Dietrich the

Three portraits for The Devil
is a Woman

The Devil is a Woman
Above: Concha Perez reaches the border, having eloped with Antonio Galvan after his duel with Don Pasqual
Left: Portrait for that film

one keeping watch over him. On a professional level, von Sternberg never recovered from their partnership. Dietrich kept going on her own, but she never forsook him in spirit, conceding even in her recent memoirs that she was indebted to him for everything.

There is something very distressing about von Sternberg's cinematographic decline – the succession of failures he was to experience in the years to come. In the days before *The Blue Angel*, von Sternberg made films prolifically and was considered one of the most talented directors of the time. Suddenly, as if he were not to be forgiven for his relationship with Dietrich, he found it harder and harder to make films. Marlene, who was much less famous than von Sternberg at the outset, was the one who emerged the stronger for their partnership. Yet neither would she escape absolutely scot-free: the next five years were not easy for her. She was never again to find the cinema as exciting, and of the twenty-seven films in which she was later involved, there are scarcely more than five or six which are of interest.

By becoming totally immersed, both intellectually and emotionally, in this venture, von Sternberg and Dietrich managed to achieve something unique. The result is that these seven films piece together to form a near-perfect whole and present us with – a rarity in the cinema – passion in its most absolute form.

It does not matter if the true version of their story comes through on screen or not. The fact that von Sternberg denies it in his memoirs does not prove anything, especially since he includes the quotation from Gauguin (see page 35). After a relationship such as this, discussion or analysis is impossible. We can all learn something from von Sternberg in these seven films. He does not do things by halves. He has recorded, forcibly and honestly, everything he felt: we see his hopes and fears, the rebellious side of his nature, his strengths and weaknesses. Above all, he was bold and lucid enough to spoil nothing by stopping just in time.

The closing image of The Devil is a Woman: *Concha Perez returns to Don Pasqual's bedside*

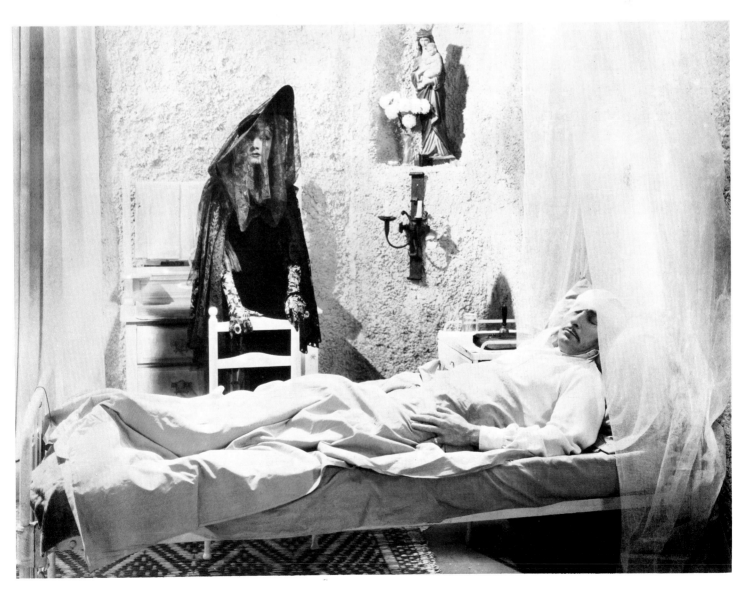

The Box Office

When I decided that I wanted mirrors to make my apartment
look bigger, some of my friends said to me, 'Mirrors? Doesn't that smack of
Hollywood?' What is so bad about Hollywood?

MARLENE DIETRICH

February 1936 saw Marlene Dietrich begin a new film with Gary Cooper, entitled *Desire*. The director was Frank Borzage and the producer Ernst Lubitsch, who was at the time Production Manager at Paramount's California studios. *Desire* is a frivolous comedy which relates how a jewel thief (Marlene Dietrich), a sort of hotel burglar, tried to con an easy-going engineer from Detroit (Gary Cooper) and falls head over heels in love with him. The tension has now vanished completely from her films, and Marlene appears to be enjoying herself. She is no longer a *femme fatale* but, rather, a woman on the make who ends up getting married and living in the comfort of a bourgeois community in Detroit.

Desire contrasts so sharply with von Sternberg's films that all the contemporary critics, speaking highly of the film, could not refrain from mentioning that their break-up seemed to constitute a change for the better. Now that von Sternberg no longer exerted a hold over her, Dietrich burst into life, bubbled with fun and could at last come into her own. People are rather too inclined to give Lubitsch the credit for *Desire*'s

Below: Desire, *1935.*
*Madeleine de Beaupré
(Marlene Dietrich) and Tom
Bradley (Gary Cooper) in
Spain*
Opposite: About the time of
Desire

I Loved a Soldier, 1936. Marlene played the part of a chambermaid in this film, which was never completed

success. It is certainly true that the producer's role then was not comparable to what it is now, though he often contributed greatly to the success of a film, intelligently matching the right director to the right actors and managing to manipulate the studios skilfully. But the director of *Desire*, Frank Borzage, is not to be dismissed lightly; the film's delicate touches, its sparkling humour, and its pace are all due in the main to him.

There is little more to be said about the film, apart from declaring that Marlene is charming throughout, Gary Cooper is just right in his role, and our attention is not for a second allowed to wander. Marlene was to remember with pleasure making this film and working with Frank Borzage.

Despite the critics' enthusiasm, the public were less than keen, and Marlene's popularity began to diminish alarmingly. But Lubitsch, with whom Marlene was then on excellent terms, was not to be discouraged, and decided straightaway to start on another film, *I Loved a Soldier*. He chose as director Henry Hathaway, who had just been enormously successful with *The Lives of a Bengal Lancer, Peter Ibbetson*, and picked Charles Boyer to play opposite Marlene.

Dating from her days with von Sternberg, Dietrich had reserved the right to voice her opinion of the screenplay – a privilege shared by very few stars, and which she insisted on maintaining, come hell or high water, in all her films. Filming had no sooner begun than Marlene expressed certain objections. The first producer, Benjamin Glazer, refused to continue in the circumstances, and Lubitsch decided to assume direct control. Filming continued but, quite patently, Dietrich did not like the screenplay; endless

debates between her and the director only served to make things worse. When Lubitsch had to leave for Europe and was replaced by a third producer, William Le Baron, the situation became impossible. At this juncture, with one month's work behind her, and the contract with Lubitsch already signed, Marlene decided to pull out. Approximately one million U.S. dollars had already been swallowed up by the production. Paramount found Margaret Sullavan as a replacement for Dietrich, but she broke a bone in her elbow at the start of the filming and the film was abandoned. *I Loved a Soldier* must rank as one of the most expensive unfinished films in the entire history of Hollywood.

All this did little to help Marlene out of her difficulties. And yet it was she who was chosen by David O. Selznick, one of the most eminent Hollywood producers and later to be responsible for *Gone With the Wind*, to play opposite Charles Boyer in *The Garden of Allah*, under the direction of Richard Boleslawski. One of the first films to be made in Technicolor, it tells the story of a beautiful, chaste lady (Marlene Dietrich) who meets

The Garden of Allah, *1936.*
Domini Enfilden (Marlene
Dietrich) with Boris
Androvsky (Charles Boyer),
the defrocked monk

and marries in the sands of the Sahara someone who she later discovers is a defrocked monk (Charles Boyer). Once this secret has been uncovered, she leads her husband back to the monastery.

Shot in the Yuma Desert, Arizona, in extremely hot conditions, the filming was a catalogue of disasters: with the exception of Marlene, everyone fell ill. It is a very ostentatious film; individual frames are almost too carefully contrived; the actors, with immaculate make-up and not a hair out of place, are dressed as if they were at a first night rather than in the middle of the desert. This implausible atmosphere emphasizes the film's superficiality. It is not possible to believe in the story line for a second; consequently, we feel distanced from the film. And yet, despite its self-consciousness and lack of credibility, it has a certain endearing fragile quality. Perhaps the fact that Boleslawski was ill throughout the filming and died a little later has something to do with this. The religious element – the denial of happiness and the theme of sacrifice –

even though clumsily interpreted, undeniably gives the film a more profound dimension. Marlene, looking ravishing from start to finish, plays the part of a woman who is too chaste by half. *The Garden of Allah* is a very odd film: neither an unmitigated disaster nor a riotous success, it is rather touching in an awkward way and does not leave a bad after-taste.

Once again, this film did not break even financially, and Marlene, accompanied by Maria, boarded the *Normandie* and left for Europe. Marlene had thirty-six pieces of luggage, gave cocktail parties most evenings in her private suite, and floated about in flamboyant pyjama suits, with her fingernails painted green to match her emeralds.

Dietrich's departure from Hollywood at this stage was inspired by Alexander Korda, who beckoned her to London where he had just breathed new life into the British film industry by founding London Films. It was something in the nature of a reunion, for

Knight Without Armour, 1937. Alexandra, the young countess, at home in St Petersburg just before her house is seized by Revolutionaries

they had already worked together in Berlin in 1926 (*A Modern Du Barry* and *Madame Wants No Children*), though in those days Marlene had been no more than a supporting actress. This time they were to make *Knight Without Armour*; the leading man was Robert Donat and the producer was a Frenchman, Jacques Feyder. The story takes place in Russia in 1917, at the height of the Revolution. It tells the tale of a young Englishman who, critical of the Tsarist regime, finds himself supporting the Bolsheviks, and falls in love with a young Russian countess. The scene is set superbly and Marlene looks dazzling. The plot moves in leaps and bounds – so that they meet, fall in love, and then are shunted between the Red Army and the White Army. This results in some very fine scenes, though we cannot help wondering what von Sternberg would have achieved in the same situation. The film seems unbalanced because it was very heavily cut during the editing process; for example, the famous scene in which Marlene's legs are exposed as she takes a bath, has not always been retained in the prints in circulation today.

That Dietrich is a generous and thoughtful person is well illustrated by a tale that is still told about the making of the film. Robert Donat had fallen seriously ill and had to stop work for a month, so Alexander Korda suggested to Dietrich that he might make Donat's role less important and give it to another actor. Marlene refused and, so that

Knight Without Armour.
Countess Alexandra has been
entrusted by the Reds to a
young Englishman (Robert
Donat)

*Disguised as peasants and
taking refuge in the forest, the
two central characters in*
Knight Without Armour
fall in love

Donat kept his part, decided to shoot all the scenes that did not involve Donat during
that critical month.

After shooting had finished, Marlene stayed in London for a short while. After taking
Maria to her boarding school in Switzerland she returned to London where she moved
into an apartment next door to Douglas Fairbanks Jr, with whom she was often seen
socially. She urged him to accept the role of Rupert of Hentzau in *The Prisoner of Zenda*,
a film he was hesitant about appearing in but which was to establish his reputation
worldwide.

Von Sternberg, meanwhile, was in the process of making *I Claudius* with Charles
Laughton and Merle Oberon, also for Alexander Korda. He and Dietrich called on each
other, but von Sternberg had many problems with Charles Laughton and *I Claudius* was
never completed. During this period Rudi, who was living in Paris with Tamara, came
to see Marlene several times.

When *Knight Without Armour* was released it was another commercial disaster, and
Dietrich joined the likes of Bette Davis and Katharine Hepburn on the box office 'poison
list'. A sort of black list drawn up very arbitrarily by the distributors, it had a definite
effect on the appeal and popularity of the actors of the day.

Knight Without Armour.
*For a short while the Whites
resume control of the area and
the Countess, now without the
young Englishman, is treated
again with due respect. But the
Reds attack again...*

Two pictures taken on the set of Angel, *1937*
Opposite: With Herbert Marshall (left) and Ernest Lubitsch (right), celebrating Lubitsch's birthday
Right: Marlene playing the violin. As a child she played expertly, but had to give up the instrument because of a wrist injury

While Marlene was in London the Germans tried to lure her back to work in her native country. In fact she had already applied for American citizenship. In 1938 Joachim von Ribbentrop, the German ambassador in London, put to her a more concrete proposition on Hitler's behalf: *The Blue Angel* was, apparently, his favourite film! She was not interested, and in 1939 she assumed American nationality. The Nazis were livid and accused her of being a traitor to her country.

After *Knight Without Armour*, Marlene returned to Hollywood to star in *Angel*, produced and directed by Ernst Lubitsch and co-starring Herbert Marshall and Melvyn Douglas. The relationship between Marlene and Lubitsch seems to have deteriorated quite considerably during the filming. Marlene's heart, we feel, was not really in the project, and Lubitsch's work, though delicately executed, comes across as being too pernickety and humourless. It is the story of the wife (Marlene Dietrich) of a titled Englishman (Herbert Marshall), who falls in love with a young American in Paris (Melvyn Douglas), quite unaware that he is a wartime friend of her husband's. Finally, though, her husband wins her back. The direction lacks bite and does not manage to strike originality into a somewhat banal story line.

Both the film and Marlene's performance were badly received by critics and public alike. Paramount cancelled her contract and she decided to leave Los Angeles, travelling via New York to join Erich Maria Remarque on the Riviera.

For more than two years Marlene left the film industry well alone, living with Remarque in London, Paris and the Hôtel du Cap in Antibes. She was obviously disillusioned by her recent experiences, and was never again to have confidence in any of the films she made. Maybe this was a counter-reaction to the enthusiasm she had felt for the cinema in the von Sternberg days. In any event, she only ever appeared on screen again either to please her friends or out of financial necessity. Marlene was now thirty-eight. She went back to spend a few days in Hollywood early in 1939, but Remarque could not bear California and they swiftly left for France again.

RETURN TO HOLLYWOOD

When she returned to the Hôtel du Cap for a second stay towards the end of 1939, where she was surrounded by a small circle of faithful friends (Joe Kennedy, the father of the future President of the U.S.A., von Sternberg, Remarque, Rudi, Tamara and Maria), Marlene was asked to play in *Dédé d'Anvers*. Had she taken the part, it would have been her first encounter with Jean Gabin.

It was then that Joe Pasternak telephoned her from Hollywood, with the suggestion that she should come and appear in a western, produced by Universal and directed by George Marshall. She would be doing it not for prestige, but to put herself back on the motion picture map. After consulting Rudi, von Sternberg and Remarque, Marlene decided to accept the offer. She did not know that Pasternak had had to fight tooth and

Destry Rides Again, 1939
Left: Portrait for that film
Opposite: Frenchy (Marlene Dietrich) drinking tea

nail to make Universal agree to take her, or that this film was the start of a second career – or that she would again, for a short time, be earning a great deal of money.

Destry Rides Again, as the film was called, was tremendously successful and provided proof of Marlene's essential versatility. She played the part of Frenchy, a bar hostess with a heart of gold. The film is excellently crafted, the actors well chosen, and the action sustained. This picture includes Marlene singing 'The Boys in the Back Room', and the highly memorable fight with Una Merkel, where both women fly for each other and give as good as they get. At the end of the film Marlene dies to save James Stewart, with whom she has fallen in love. The action, the humour, and sentimentality of the film, and the new image projected by Marlene – who is more vibrant and more sophisticated than ever – fired the public with enthusiasm. Overnight Marlene became first-class box officer material once again, and Joe Pasternak decided to begin another project: it became *Seven Sinners*.

At that moment war broke out in Europe. Marlene, despite her new-found success, was extremely worried and never ceased doing everything within her power to help the victims of the war. So she settled in New York for a short while and, together with Billy Wilder and Ernst Lubitsch, helped refugees to settle by trying to find them work: the writer Thomas Mann was one such person. According to Marlene's memoirs, she and her colleagues even built up a network of agents, which saved the lives of hundreds of people by enabling them to go through Switzerland.

Destry Rides Again.
Before, during and after the fight with Lilybelle Callahan (Una Merkel). Tom Destry (James Stewart) separates the two women by pouring a bucket of cold water over them.

SEVEN SINNERS

When Joe Pasternak asked Tay Garnett, whom he wanted to direct Marlene in *Seven Sinners*, if he could find a suitable male lead, Tay suggested John Wayne – a young actor who had already made his mark, thanks to John Ford, but who was as yet no more than a potential big name. Pasternak approved the idea, but then remembered that he needed Dietrich's approval, so Tay Garnett and John Wayne arranged to meet in Universal Studios' canteen. On the agreed day, Tay arrived with Marlene Dietrich. He was, of course, already a Hollywood veteran; his first silent films went back to 1926 and he had reached the peak of his career at the start of the 1930s; even so, he was only six years Marlene's senior. Whenever Marlene appeared in a public place it caused something of a stir, and this was no exception. As Tay and Marlene came in together, John Wayne was standing by the door. Marlene walked straight past him and headed for her table. Tay followed her. Then, just as she was about to sit down, she turned round and, pointing to John Wayne, whispered to Tay: 'Daddy, buy me that!'

Seven Sinners is the story of Bijou (Marlene Dietrich), a cabaret singer who has been deported from islands in the South Pacific because of the disruption she causes wherever she goes. Escorted by her two bodyguards, Little Ned (Broderick Crawford), an absent-minded sailor who has deserted the Navy, and Sascha (Mischa Auer), a conjuror and pickpocket, Marlene steps ashore on the island of Boni-Komba to go back to a former haunt, the Seven Sinners' café, and her former boss, Tony (Billy Gilbert). She falls in love with an officer in the Navy (John Wayne), but, refusing to jeopardize his career by marrying him, she takes her leave, though not without having provoked a magnificent fight first. On the cargo boat which carries her away she meets for the second time a doctor who had fallen in love with her at the beginning of the film, and who was waiting for her. She then tries to start a new life with him.

Seven Sinners is one of the rare films in which Marlene has the lead role and gives a polished performance, even though it is in quite a different register from the films made with von Sternberg. No doubt this stems partly from the combined talents of Tay Garnett and Marlene Dietrich, and partly from the fact that they worked in perfect harmony with each other. Tay, in sharp contrast with von Sternberg, was a straightforward man; he was spontaneous, warm-hearted and totally unsophisticated. Dietrich quickly learned what Tay expected from her, and was able to adjust effortlessly to him as a person. Such excellent results spring from the privileged relationship between actor and director, as has been noted before. Marlene was very sensitive to Tay Garnett's talent for lending a surprising sense of dignity to the supporting characters. Take, for example, Broderick Crawford, Marlene's bodyguard. Throughout the film

Seven Sinners, 1940
Left, above: Bijou (Marlene Dietrich), with naval support, sings 'The Man's in the Navy'.
Right, above: Playing the musical saw with Tony (Billy Gilbert), proprietor of the Seven Sinners night club, and Sascha (Mischa Auer), the kleptomaniac. This picture is either a still, or a scene which was later edited out of the film
Opposite: A portrait for Seven Sinners

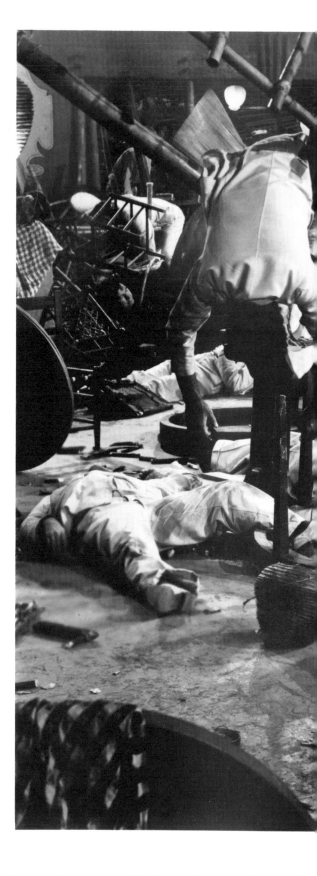

Seven Sinners
Above, top and bottom: Little Ned (Broderick Crawford), a deserter from the Navy, dares to hit Bijou for the first time in his life, having heard that she might coerce an officer (John Wayne) to desert
Right, above: The final fight, with Bijou in the centre

he is prepared to let himself be killed in order to save Marlene. But in a burst of unexpected violence he goes so far as to hit her when he fears she will lure the navy officer away from his duty, and accuses her of failing to understand exactly what the Navy means to a sailor (he, of course, being a deserter, knows full well!)

Marlene plays along with this all the way. We sense a certain affectionate, harmonious complicity between her and the minor characters: the kleptomaniac magician, Sascha, Tony, the proprietor of the Seven Sinners' café, and, of course, Little Ned. We might even go so far as to say that the love interest between John Wayne and Marlene becomes of secondary importance, and that we are more concerned with all these lesser details than with the intrigue proper.

Tay Garnett also cocks a snook at von Sternberg: he dresses Marlene in outrageous clothes and plays on light and shade, using veils and smokescreens and deliberately ridiculous décors. If by any stroke of luck we are able to see a good print of the film, we cannot help but admire how diligently Tay Garnett, aided by that great cameraman Rudolph Mate, sets about the task of maintaining the aesthetic quality of the image. There are many wonderful moments to be enjoyed in *Seven Sinners*, and it must surely rank as one of the best films made by Marlene and Tay Garnett. At the time it was an unqualified success. When filming had finished, Marlene lavished presents on every member of the film crew; Tay Garnett himself received a gold watch, engraved with her name.

The Flame of New Orleans,
1941
Right: As Claire Ledeux
Below: With René Clair on
the set
Right, below: Claire Ledeux
kisses Robert Latour (Bruce
Cabot) in one of the rare shots
in which Marlene Dietrich is
seen to kiss someone

*Above: Claire Ledeux faints
during her wedding to Charles
Giraud (Roland Young) in*
The Flame of New
Orleans

Understandably encouraged by his two earlier successes, Joe Pasternak decided to
keep going. This time he asked René Clair to direct Marlene in *The Flame of New
Orleans*. René Clair had become an expatriate, having escaped from occupied France,
and Pasternak had immediately signed him up. Yet the combination of Marlene and
René Clair does not live up to expectations. *The Flame of New Orleans* works well on
an aesthetic level, and carries the René Clair mark with its almost ridiculous attention
to minute detail and its characteristic precision of style. However, whether René Clair
was not yet attuned to America and its system of producing films, or whether Marlene's
personality disorientated him, *The Flame of New Orleans* does not allow Marlene the
scope to give an exceptional performance.

Manpower, *1941*
Two contemporary portraits.
Opposite, above: Fay Duval
(Marlene Dietrich) after her
husband Hank McHenry
(Edward G. Robinson) suffers
an accident at work. On
Hank's left is his best friend,
Johnny Marshall (George
Raft), with whom Fay has
fallen in love
Opposite, below: Fay alone
in her apartment

Despite the less than warm reception given to René Clair's film by the public, Warner Bros still decided to ask Marlene to appear in a film called *Manpower*, co-starring Edward G. Robinson and George Raft, both very good old friends of Marlene's, and directed by Raoul Walsh. Here again the combination of Walsh and Dietrich is somewhat disappointing. It is essentially a film about men, and Marlene as *femme fatale* merely provides the female intrigue. When Walsh concentrates on the friendship between the two men the film is good, but as soon as Marlene appears on screen, the film's interest decreases. We are left with the impression that Marlene's role is totally superfluous.

The Spoilers, *1942. Alex McNamara (Randolph Scott), Isabelle (Marietta Canty), and Cherry Mallotte (Marlene Dietrich)*

Opposite, above and below:
The Lady is Willing, *1942. Elizabeth Madden (Marlene Dietrich) with baby Corey (Davy Joseph James)*

All the enjoyment Marlene derived from the cinema again during the time of *Destry Rides Again* and *Seven Sinners* quickly evaporated. However, during the summer of 1942 she made three more films: *The Lady is Willing*, directed by Mitchell Leisen, an old friend of hers; *The Spoilers*, directed by Ray Enright, with John Wayne and Randolph Scott; and *Pittsburgh*, directed by Lewis Seiler, with the same actors. *The Lady is Willing* is a comedy in which Marlene plays the part of a famous singer of light opera who wants to adopt a baby which has been found abandoned. Although Marlene plays well, the film is not of particular interest. One day, as she was holding the baby in her arms, she tripped over a cable, and because she fell awkwardly so as to protect the child she broke her ankle. Leisen suggested to her that they should stop the filming, but Marlene would not hear of it and, without so much as a murmur of complaint, she completed the film. *The Spoilers* and *Pittsburgh* are two competently executed action films in which Marlene plays very professionally.

Above: Pittsburgh, *1942.*
Marlene Dietrich in her
dressing-room
Below: Hollywood
Parade, *1944. With*
Orson Welles

Opposite: A portrait for
Pittsburgh

Kismet, 1944
Left, above: For this film
Marlene's legs were painted
gold. It took two coats to
achieve the right effect, and
each application lasted an hour
under the supervision of
M.G.M.'s make-up artist,
Edith Wilson.

Left, below: Jack Coke, an
expert in eastern dance,
instructs Marlene
Above: The dance of Jamilla
(Marlene Dietrich), the queen
of the Baghdad dancers, in
Kismet

But Marlene was growing weary of the stereotyped image thrust upon her. In the next five years her contact with the cinema was minimal, though in 1944 she appeared for old times' sake in two films. The first was *Follow the Boys*, in which she is cut in half in a stunt by Orson Welles. This film is a lavish extravaganza, a sort of Hollywood homage to all the artists who had dedicated themselves to entertaining the Allied troops. The second was *Kismet*, directed by William Dieterle with whom she had appeared in *Man by the Roadside* (*Der Mensch am Wege*) in Germany in 1923. Marlene had a slightly larger role in this picture and performed a spectacular dance with her long legs painted gold.

Jamilla's dance in Kismet

1

2

3

4

5

When the filming of *Kismet* was completed, Marlene placed her acting talents at the service of the American Army. This was the start of what she described as 'the most extraordinary adventure' she was ever to be involved in, and it left a considerable mark on her. Her attitude to the cinema and to life in general altered quite radically. She was to appear again in very few films, and she became more and more involved with her family. It was just after the war, she reveals in her memoirs, that she lost her faith completely.

It is certainly noticeable that most of the parts she took in the following years were character roles of a more complex, less superficial, nature. She frequently portrayed women inextricably caught up in problematic situations springing from the war and relating to Germany, such as in *A Foreign Affair, Witness for the Prosecution* and *Judgement at Nuremberg.*

The War and After

They came to see me and told me: 'There are some Nazis over there and they're ill. Would you mind going and speaking to them in German?' So I went to see these young Nazis with their pale complexions and they inquired, 'Are you the real Marlene Dietrich?' When I said I was, all was forgiven and I sang 'Lili Marlene' for everyone in the hospital. It was the best moment in my life.

MARLENE DIETRICH

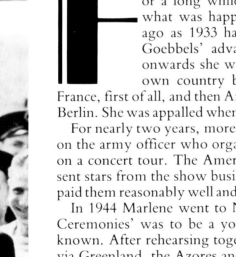

For a long while, Marlene Dietrich had been desperately concerned by what was happening in Europe. Hitler's acquisition of power as long ago as 1933 had weighed heavily on her; then, later, there had been Goebbels' advances and von Ribbentrop's propositions. From 1932 onwards she was permanently reminded of what was happening in her own country by the constant stream of refugees which flowed into France, first of all, and then America; among them were several of her own friends from Berlin. She was appalled when war broke out and German troops invaded France.

For nearly two years, more or less from Pearl Harbor onwards, Marlene put pressure on the army officer who organized the troops' entertainments to send her to the front on a concert tour. The American Army had a highly organized system and regularly sent stars from the show business world to the front to entertain the soldiers; they also paid them reasonably well and covered their families in the event of death.

In 1944 Marlene went to New York to discuss the plan of action. Her 'Master of Ceremonies' was to be a young actor called Danny Thomas, who was as yet little known. After rehearsing together in New York, they left in a military plane and flew via Greenland, the Azores and Casablanca before finally arriving in Algiers. There, in the Opera House, they put on their first show.

They had been advised to be careful: the soldiers were often fed-up – they could easily get over-excited and start throwing whatever came to hand. In the event, everything went smoothly, and the soldiers were absolutely enchanted by Dietrich. When, three-

Opposite
Above: Taking the oath of allegiance to become an American citizen, 1938
Centre: With her daughter at El Morocco in New York in 1942–3
Below: Welcoming troops back
from the war on 20 July 1945
Left
Above: Signing autographs for G.I.s in Germany, 1945
Below: With Jean Gabin and the French Navy in North Africa, 1944

quarters of the way through the show, a bomb exploded nearby and the power was cut off, the organizers wanted to stop the show. But Marlene went on singing, and light was provided by the soldiers' cigarette lighters.

Thanks to Danny Thomas, and the sort of difficult audiences she often encountered, Marlene learnt a great many things which were to stand her in good stead when she decided in the late 1950s to do her own concert tours: she learnt how to gauge the mood of a theatre audience and how to win its affection – things which involve not only talent but also a certain degree of professionalism.

Marlene's tour continued in Italy. She travelled light with one small suitcase, wore uniform, ate with the officers, and sang in open-air improvised theatres in the pouring rain, as well as in military hospitals. Of course, she was showered with flowers and presents: all these gifts were much cherished.

As she travelled, she attempted to gather as much information as possible about her family, and it was on one of these trips that she learnt that Goebbels had had her sister

imprisoned. On 6 June 1944 she was in Rome when it was liberated. She wrote many letters to Jean Gabin, who was at this time driving tanks in North Africa. In Bari, Italy, she became seriously ill: her recovery was partly due to treatment with penicillin, which had been discovered not many years before by Alexander Fleming – her affection for and gratitude towards him date from these days. In the same year, when she was in the Ardennes, her hands were severely frostbitten: she has had to suffer from the after-effects ever since.

On 16 June she returned to New York with her travelling companions and, despite the fact that she was exhausted, gave several interviews. In early September she went back to Europe and continued touring. On this tour she made the acquaintance of General Patton, Commander of the 3rd American Army, who admired her courage and sent her to several strategic bases.

The Nazis, meanwhile, were furious with her for undertaking these tours, and indeed most Germans resented the fact that she had been so very active. They made their point fifteen years later when Marlene sang in Berlin for the first time in many years. On one occasion Marlene was scared out of her wits when the detachment in which she was serving was surrounded; she was very nearly captured and knew that she risked death. General James Gavin saved her just in time and took her back to Paris.

Marlene went to Paris in late 1945 and took an apartment in Avenue Montaigne, where she still lives. In mid-September, for the first time in thirteen years, she returned to Berlin, where she saw her mother and her friends again, a reunion which proved a distressing emotional experience set against a backcloth of devastation. Next followed the brief stay in Biarritz, cut short by the death of her mother, with whom she had only just been reunited. On her return to Paris she saw a great deal of the Hemingways, and in late 1945 and early 1946 Marlene spent most of her time in Paris with Gabin. She also saw Jean Cocteau again, whom she had met in Hollywood and admired tremendously. He wanted her to play the part of Death in *Orphée*, but the plan fell through.

Martin Roumagnac, 1946. Blanche Ferrand (Marlene Dietrich) and Martin Roumagnac (Jean Gabin)

Even though she was earning good money and her tours guaranteed her much favourable publicity, it took guts on Marlene's part to embark, aged over forty, on such a terrifying venture, quite irrespective of the fact that her nationality by birth was often a handicap. She had left her homeland at the age of thirty and found herself supporting the other side in war because of her beliefs. She had seen the country of her birth crushed and been made aware of all the evil for which it had been responsible. No wonder she was now left feeling shaken and unsure. The dignity and generosity that Marlene managed to maintain in the face of all this surely merit all the more praise.

Marlene Dietrich and Jean Gabin were brought closer together by the Liberation of France – a historical event which they witnessed practically side by side – and for a while, one was never without the other. When the Marcel Carné and Jacques Prévert project

Golden Earrings, 1947
Left: Signing autographs.
Right: Colonel Ralph
Denistoun (Ray Milland) and
Lydia (Marlene Dietrich) vow
to meet again in the same place
as soon as the war is over

failed to materialize, they embarked on another film, *Martin Roumagnac*, directed by Georges Lacombe. The first film Marlene made in French, it was a flop in both France and the U.S.A.

Georges Lacombe directs in a spiritless fashion, while Marlene and Gabin seem ill at ease. Seeing it again today we might hope to find something we previously overlooked, but we are still left feeling dissatisfied. All the same, it is amusing to watch the way Marlene changes in such a French setting and to hear her speak another language.

Once they had finished shooting *Martin Roumagnac*, the relationship between Dietrich and Gabin deteriorated. When Mitchell Leisen, with whom she had already made *The Lady is Willing*, telephoned with another project for her, Marlene went back to Hollywood. The film was to be *Golden Earrings*, and in it Marlene had to play a gypsy.

A Foreign Affair, *1948*
Left: With John Lund
*Left, below: With Jean Arthur
and Billy Wilder*
*Below: With Billy Wilder and
John Lund*
*Opposite: Erika von
Schluetow (Marlene Dietrich)
with Hans Otto Birgel (Peter
von Zerneck), being received
by Adolf Hitler (Bobby
Watson) at the Berlin
Opera House*

Paramount had been reluctant at first, but Leisen persuaded them otherwise and the result surprised everyone. Telling the story of an English spy (Ray Milland) whose life is saved by a gypsy and who, six years later, arranges to meet her, duly sees her again and goes off with her in her gypsy caravan, the film is made with great style in the Hollywood historical film tradition. With jet-black hair and a smooth complexion, eating chunks of raw fish and singing Hungarian folk songs, her gypsy caravan in the background, Marlene carries off the part of the passionate, possessive and devoted gypsy with apparent effortlessness and touches of humour.

The critics of the day thought that this new Dietrich image would not go down too well with the public, but despite their fears the film was enormously successful. Yet the shooting itself had not gone very well. First of all there was a clash of personalities between Ray Milland and Dietrich. On top of this, a strike was called and Paramount issued instructions to all those involved in the film to sleep on the set so as not to have to cross the picket lines.

A Foreign Affair
Opposite: Erika von Schluetow and Captain John Pringle (John Lund)
Left, above: Erika von Schluetow appearing at the Lorelei night club. Playing the part of the pianist is Frederick Hollander himself, the composer of Marlene's songs since The Blue Angel

But the film's success was not enough to lure Marlene back to the cinema. She was very busy with her daughter and her first grandson. She also did some work for radio, feeling that it allowed her more independence and the freedom to do as she liked; she dabbled a little in television, but did not feel at all at ease with the medium. Marlene continued to commute between Paris and Los Angeles, and in Washington she was awarded the *Légion d'Honneur* by the ambassador to France.

In late 1947 her friend Billy Wilder asked her to play the part of a one-time Nazi in *A Foreign Affair*, co-starring Jean Arthur and John Lund. So, eighteen years after *The Blue Angel*, she was back again in Berlin, playing the part of a cabaret singer. The role was a difficult one and she hesitated over accepting it for some time, but in the event she coped magnificently. Wilder succeeds perfectly in conveying the uncertain and uneasy atmosphere of the days following the war by maintaining the tension and undercutting it with humour. Wilder is one of the few directors to have directed Marlene really well – something which may have stemmed from the fact that they were good friends. Frederick Hollander, the composer of her best songs in the films after *The Blue*

Jigsaw, 1949. The head
waiter (Henry Fonda), the
night club proprietor (Fletcher
Markle, the film's director),
and a guest (Marlene
Dietrich)

Angel, accompanies her on the piano as she performs two fine numbers, 'Black Market' and 'Illusions'. Marlene does not play the lead, but in two or three splendid scenes, where she appears with a very American Jean Arthur, she puts over with tremendous sensitivity and discretion the difficulties experienced in Germany. *A Foreign Affair* ranks among the five best films that Dietrich made without von Sternberg.

For the next two years Marlene made no films, apart from appearing very briefly in *Jigsaw* because she was a friend of the director Fletcher Markle and his wife, Mercedes McCambridge. She continued working for radio and looking after her family, and about this time she became friendly with Edith Piaf. Then in 1950 Alfred Hitchcock invited her to go to London to play a famous singer and actress in his film *Stage Fright*. Marlene accepted instantly.

François Truffaut, in his book based on a series of interviews with Hitchcock, briefly touches on *Stage Fright*. Hitchcock actually acknowledges that the film does not work, chiefly because of a misleading flashback which dramatically puts the audience on the wrong track. It is stating the obvious to say that Marlene Dietrich is as out of place in a Hitchcock film as in one of Truffaut's. Here again she does not have the lead role, but

Stage Fright, *1950*
Opposite, above: Charlotte Inwood (Marlene Dietrich), having just sung 'La Vie en rose', passes out at the sight of a child bringing her a bloodstained doll
Opposite, below: With Hector McGregor and Alfred Hitchcock on the set

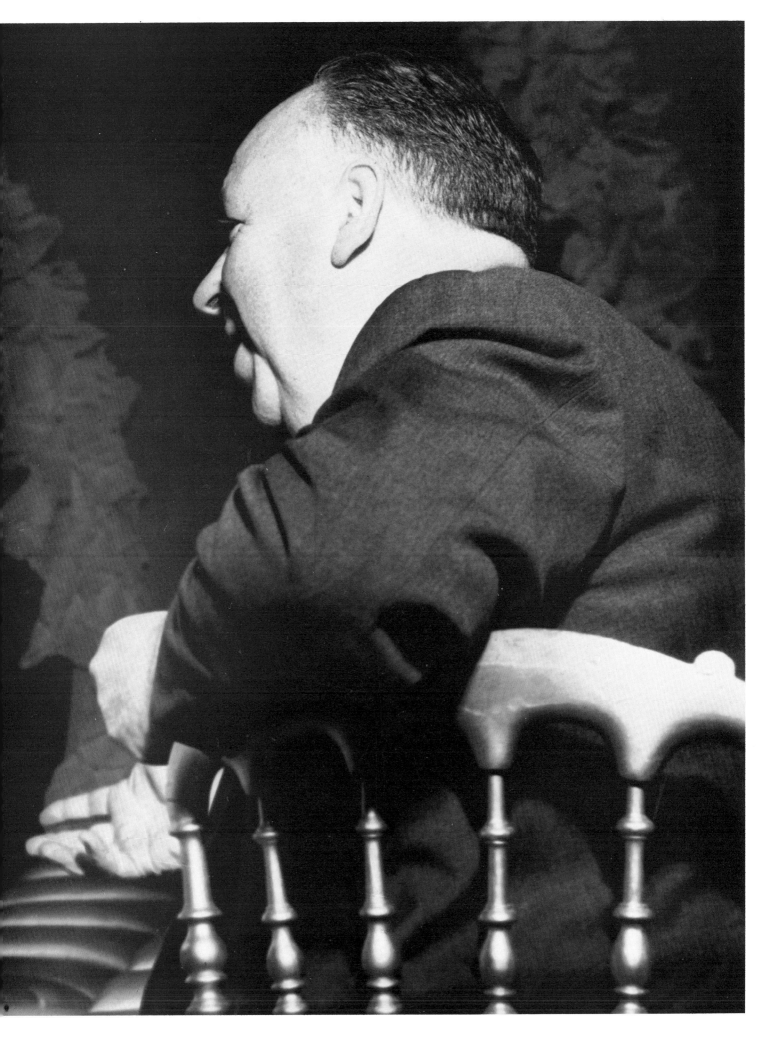

No Highway, 1951. Monica
Teasdale (Marlene Dietrich),
a musical comedy star, and Mr
Homey (James Stewart), a
young aeronautics technician

she is very much involved with the misleading flashback since Hitchcock uses it to
implicate her. From here onwards, *Stage Fright*, though it may be one of Hitchcock's
lesser films, does all the same manage to bring out the best in Marlene. The last scene,
in which she is sitting inside the theatre beside a policeman, is very fine, and contains
one remarkable close-up of Marlene. Hitchcock knew how to play cleverly on Marlene's
ambiguity and sensibility. Perhaps, in the final analysis, *Stage Fright* is not such a bad
Hitchcock film after all.

Having been back to America to help her daughter with her television career and to
look after the children, Marlene returned to England in 1951 for another film with James
Stewart, directed by Henry Koster, entitled *No Highway*. She did not like the screenplay
or the role, but resigned herself to the part out of financial necessity. The character she
plays is quite a minor one: once again she is a show business personality, but this time
she does not sing. *No Highway* is a prime example of a film about which there is little
to say, but in which Marlene gives her character a degree of credibility and undeniable
poignancy. Even though she was now over fifty, Marlene was still extremely beautiful
and the last word in elegance – she wears clothes designed by Dior throughout the entire
film. Yet again, she furnishes evidence of her talents as an actress.

With Fritz Lang in
Hollywood, 1936

Finally, in 1952, Marlene got together with one of her compatriots, her old friend Fritz Lang, for a western called *Rancho Notorious*; Arthur Kennedy and Mel Ferrer also co-starred in the film. The colour photography is superb but Marlene's talents are not really used to full advantage, and the whole is disappointing. It is a pity that there was no opportunity to make a detective film or psychological drama instead – Marlene would then have been much better able to fulfil the aims of this great director.

For five years Marlene made no more films, but was still working in radio. She set Rudi up in his ranch in 1953 and in the same year donned a lion-tamer's costume for a gala charity performance in Madison Square Garden. Now fifty-two, Marlene was in fact preparing to begin a new career. She came back, so to speak, to her first love, but this time, with many years of varied experience behind her, she needed no director to help.

Rancho Notorious, 1952
Opposite, above: Altar Keane (Marlene Dietrich), an infamous saloon bar entertainer, cornered by Deputy Sheriff Warner (Stan Jolley) and Sherriff Hardy (Lane Chandler)
Opposite, below: With Fritz Lang on the set

130

Show Business

The pictures in the papers of the dress I wore in Las Vegas weren't good. It wasn't see-through at all; it was those flashlights, they make things see-through. They could even make a thick black sweater see-through.

MARLENE DIETRICH

 arlene began her first big show in Las Vegas in December 1953. It lasted three weeks and she was paid $30,000 a week. She sang a number of songs from her films, accompanied by an orchestra conducted by Burt Bacharach who, throughout the first half of her new career, arranged and composed new material for her. Marlene did everything – production, lighting, and costumes – herself. It was in Las Vegas that she wore for the first time the infamous dress which raised eyebrows for two reasons: firstly, its exorbitant price, and secondly, because it was virtually see-through.

Her show, at least in the 1950s, was usually divided into two. For the whole of the first part, looking very feminine in dresses growing progressively more outrageous, Marlene sang her quiet, romantic numbers. Then, in the second part, she appeared wearing top hat and tails, or shorts to show off her celebrated legs, still stunning though she was now fifty-five, and, either on her own or surrounded by a female chorus, sang her most ambiguous and provocative numbers.

She first sang in London in 1954, when she was asked to appear at the Café de Paris and Noël Coward acted as host. She was a resounding success. Marlene went on to travel all over Europe. She appeared in Amsterdam, where she made a visit to Anne Frank's house a priority; she went to Monte Carlo, where she was hosted by Jean Marais who read the famous Cocteau speech (see page 11), and gave a special performance to raise money for polio sufferers in France; she returned to London shortly afterwards and went on playing to packed houses every night.

Two men figure prominently in this period of Marlene's life. First of all there was her inseparable musical arranger, Burt Bacharach who, without a shadow of a doubt, was largely responsible for Marlene's comeback. They split up as soon as he started to become famous, and when he later married Angie Dickinson Marlene held it against him. The other man was the flamboyant and brilliant producer, Mike Todd, who had divorced Joan Blondell in 1950; Marlene had a tiny part in his mammoth production, *Around the World in Eighty Days* (1956). She was deeply distressed when, in 1958, Todd was killed in New Mexico in his private plane, *The Lucky Liz*, named after his new wife Elizabeth Taylor.

Marlene still remained good friends with the Hemingways. It is also said that she was often seen with Yul Brynner and that, by persuading him to shave his head, she helped him to obtain the part of the king in *The King and I*. In the late 1950s Marlene appeared in three films, of which two at least are excellent. First of all, she made her one and only Italian film for Samuel A. Taylor, playing opposite Vittorio de Sica: made in 1957, it was called *The Monte Carlo Story*. Despite these two big names, this story of two inveterate gamblers fails to gain our attention due to its weak screenplay and poor photography. The second film is very important for Marlene and the third is unforgettable, despite Marlene's appearance being far too brief.

Billy Wilder directs, and Charles Laughton and Tyrone Power co-star, in *Witness for the Prosecution*, based on an Agatha Christie play which had already been a great stage success. Charles Laughton is, as always, excellent, and so is Tyrone Power – but Marlene gives a better performance than she had for a long time. Once again, she is cast in the role of a cabaret singer, a German lady married to an Englishman. From the moment she appears on screen she does not put a foot wrong. We can see why the lawyer (Charles Laughton) is bewitched by her. Throughout the film we are intrigued by the character she plays; she manages to lend her part just the right degree of severity, frostiness and ambivalence while remaining mysteriously disturbing. And when, at the end of the film, having undergone a radical *volte-face*, she breaks down and sobs in front of the court, the scene is particularly moving. Wilder manages to make Marlene create a properly rounded character, rather than merely playing up her own personality – for Marlene this was something new. In any case the film proves, should anyone still be in doubt, that Marlene is a remarkable actress.

At the Sahara Hotel in Las Vegas for her second show, wearing the famous dress, valued at $6000, created by Jean-Louis de la Columbia

In 1958, motivated by her affection and admiration for Orson Welles, she took a small part in *Touch of Evil*. She appears in four sequences, each time with Orson Welles. Although some critics might disagree, it is an extraordinary film: it conveys the atmosphere of a town on the Mexican border (the entire film was shot in Santa Monica, California), offers some amazing shots (especially the one which opens the film – one of the longest in the history of the cinema), and of course Orson Welles himself. It is extraordinary, too, to watch two giants of the cinema face to face. Welles is overweight, scruffy and unshaven, in the role of a highly dubious policeman, while Dietrich, as a gypsy, has become a brunette once again, and looks incredibly youthful for fifty-seven. They play former lovers, and when with her he behaves rather like a small child, in sharp contrast with his behaviour in the rest of the film. We get the impression that, in each of the sequences where they appear together on the screen, the story line (and the film) is frozen. He really does seem to have enormous respect for her and at the end of the film, when Marlene, standing by Orson Welles' dead body, delivers the line, 'What does it matter what you say about people?', we sense in her voice immense affection and much respect for the character.

'When I've seen him and talked with him, I feel like a plant that has been watered. His brilliant mind is coupled with a simple and practical heart. And he is generous with both.' Thus Dietrich describes Orson Welles in her *ABC*, which is a dictionary of thoughts and jottings. She also devotes five pages of her memoirs to his captivating personality.

With Jean-Pierre Aumont and Jean Cocteau at the Théâtre de l'Etoile in Paris, November 1959

On stage at the Théâtre de l'Etoile, November 1959

Right through the 1950s Marlene persevered with her new career. She went back several times to Las Vegas and visited South America where in Rio de Janeiro and Buenos Aires the crowds went berserk. As well as this, Marlene attended a retrospective season of her films at the Museum of Modern Art in New York in 1959.

1960 was the year when she went back to sing in Germany. As mentioned earlier, many Germans – even those who had not been particularly pro-Nazi – harboured feelings of rancour towards Marlene for her activities during the war. When she decided to go and sing in Berlin, the reception she received was, at first, decidedly frosty. She even received anonymous threats on her life, and she attracted a lukewarm reception in Hamburg. In the end, however, the atmosphere grew more relaxed, and in Berlin, as elsewhere, people swarmed to come and hear her.

The other major event of 1960 took place in Israel. The authorities had forbidden her to sing in German, but in Tel Aviv, when the show was in full swing, she started a song in her native language. This made her an even greater success, and she received one of the longest standing ovations in her whole career, lasting a full thirty-five minutes! She was to do the same in Jerusalem. The Israelis had doubtless not forgotten the stand Marlene had taken against her own country, and all the efforts she had made to help the refugees flocking to the U.S.A. from Europe.

Her private life suffered a setback following Ernest Hemingway's suicide and the deaths of her friends Gary Cooper, Gérard Philipe, and Jean Cocteau, and Marlene determined never to attend a funeral again. However, her professional life went from strength to strength, and her tours took her all over the world. In 1963 she went to

Left, above: With Orson Welles and Michel Simon at the Théâtre de l'Etoile, 1959
Above: With Maria Schell and General de Gaulle at a gala performance held at the Palais de Chaillot, 1960
Opposite: Taking a bow at the Théâtre de l'Etoile, November 1959

London where she performed at the Prince of Wales Theatre before H.M. Queen Elizabeth, The Queen Mother. The following year she was hugely successful in Russia and was deeply touched by the standing ovation given her by the crowd, who were on their feet for half an hour. 1965 saw her in South Africa, Sweden and Norway and returning to England, where she toured several major cities including Liverpool, Bristol, Brighton and Manchester. In October that year she went to Australia for the first time and appeared in Melbourne. Everywhere she went she was highly acclaimed.

She had not, however, completely abandoned the cinema: in 1961 Stanley Kramer asked her to play the part of the widow of a German general in *Judgment at Nuremberg*. Marlene was fired with enthusiasm, not only by the role itself, but also at the thought of playing opposite Spencer Tracy, for she regarded him as one of the very greatest actors of the screen.

It was a large-scale production which won many Oscars and co-starred Montgomery Clift, Judy Garland, Burt Lancaster, and Richard Widmark. This star-studded line-up does give the film a certain stamp of quality, but detracts rather from its credibility. It was Marlene's last major role on screen.

In 1962 Marlene did the voice-over on a documentary film about Hitler, entitled *Black Fox* and directed by Louis Clyde Stoumen. By removing all trace of emotion from her voice Marlene makes this an extremely moving documentary, and the film was awarded an Oscar. She threw herself into the job in a wholly selfless fashion.

Motivated by her friendship with its star, Audrey Hepburn, Marlene made a very brief appearance in *Paris When It Sizzles* (1964), which amounted to her getting out of

Left, above: Rehearsing for a show at the Olympia, April 1962
Above: A recording session in the early 1950s
Opposite: Paris, 1962

a white Rolls Royce, clad in a white dress, and going into the House of Dior. In the same year, just after the Edinburgh Festival, she split up with Burt Bacharach. 1967 found her appearing on Broadway for the first time and in 1968 she went back to Australia. At about this time she appeared in some advertisements for an airline company, revealing her legs which were as stunning as ever.

Von Sternberg died in 1969: Marlene was in New York at the time. Von Sternberg's wife, Merri, broke the news to her and people were surprised that Marlene did not attend the funeral. However, when Merri got home afterwards Marlene was waiting to comfort her.

Marlene, now in her seventieth year, was still working, though her pace was slower. In 1972 she made her first show for British television, directed by Alexander Cohen. She gave two concerts the following year at L'Espace Cardin in Paris: the first night was somewhat chaotic as she was hounded by photographers, but the second went much more smoothly and Marlene was showered with flowers. She also appeared for a season at the Grosvenor House in London.

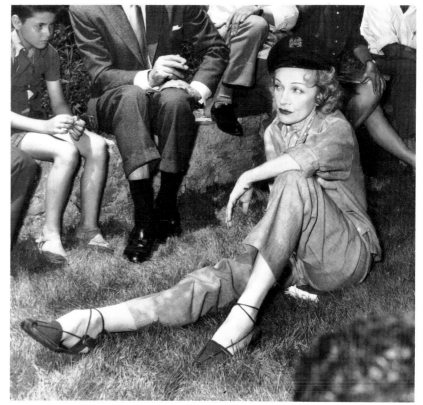

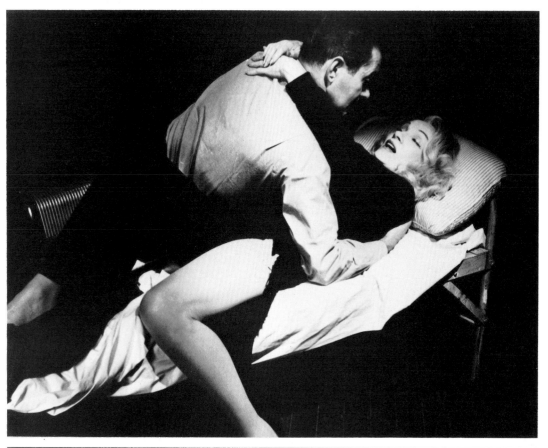

Witness for the Prosecution,
*1958. Christine and Leonard
Vole (Marlene Dietrich and
Tyrone Power) in Germany
just after the war*

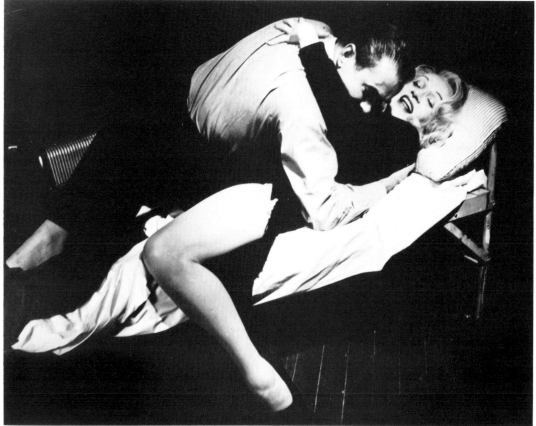

*Opposite: Christine Vole
giving evidence at her
husband's trial in* Witness for
the Prosecution

However, for a long time her luck appeared to have run out. In Washington, as she went to congratulate the conductor, she fell into the orchestra pit, and for a while she had to be pushed everywhere in a wheelchair. Then she broke her right leg in her Paris apartment. Eighteen months later, in September 1975, she broke her left hip after a performance in Australia.

Rudi died in June 1976, and Jean Gabin in November that year. Most of Marlene's time now was devoted to writing her memoirs in her Avenue Montaigne apartment. Around this time the title role of Fedora in Billy Wilder's film was offered to her, but she turned it down. In 1978 she was involved for three days in the making of a film by David Hemmings, *Just a Gigolo*, with Kim Novak, David Bowie, and Curt Jurgens. Marlene plays a Prussian baroness in charge of a group of gigolos, and she sings the song, 'Just a Gigolo'.

Her memoirs, published in Germany in 1979, contain no earth-shattering revelations and the book did not exactly cause a sensation. She confines herself to relating encounters with the famous; she speaks about her friends and squashes a number of stories which had been told about her. It is, however, a very well written book, like von Sternberg's own memoirs, and confirms that she is a cultured, intelligent, and sensitive individual.

So, once again, Marlene was back in the forefront of the news. She was asked to star in plays and authors wrote parts for her, but she always turned down the offers. There was a possibility of her making another film with Billy Wilder, but the plan fell through. Despite her rekindled relationship with Germany, she never really managed to forgive her country completely. She did not enjoy post-war German literature and, no doubt because she had been in the U.S.A. during the most critical moments of the war, she found it difficult to accept and understand the twentieth-century German mentality.

This book attempts to shatter the stereotyped yet persisting image of Marlene – the myth that she is a cold, hard woman. It is vital that the future generations who, in every corner of the world, will watch and enjoy her films, understand that there is more to Marlene Dietrich than her talents as an actress and those famous legs: they must be made aware of her love of life, her energy in the face of life's trials and tribulations, her enquiring, insatiable mind, the determination with which she tackled her work, and her unstinting loyalty.

With Charles Laughton, Tyrone Power and Billy Wilder on the set of Witness for the Prosecution
Opposite
Left: Rehearsing the telephone call scene in Witness for the Prosecution
Right: Marlene disguised as a cockney in a scene from that film

WP-112-9

-10

-11

WP-106-5

-6

-7

Touch of Evil, 1958
Above: As the madame of a
bordello and former mistress
of Hank Quinlan (Orson
Welles), a neurotic, bigoted
policeman
Left: Hank Quinlan deserts
his colleagues, drawn by the
music of his former mistress

Judgment at Nuremberg,
1961
Above: The judge, Dan
Haywood (Spencer Tracy),
and Frau Bertholt (Marlene
Dietrich), a German general's
widow
Right: A portrait for that
film

Black Fox, *1962. In New*
York with Louis Clyde
Stoumen, doing the voice-over
on the film

Above: Paris When It
Sizzles, *1964. Marlene as one
of Christian Dior's customers*
Right: Just a Gigolo, *1978.
As the Prussian baroness*

At the Olympia, Paris, April 1962
Opposite: In Copenhagen in the 1960s

Ernest Hemingway knew Marlene Dietrich well, and understood her perhaps better than anyone. Let him have the last say:

I am never happier than when I've written something that I know is good, and she reads it and likes it. I value her opinion more than the critics', for she knows about the things I speak of in my books, that's to say, people, the countryside, life and death, and matters of honour and behaviour. I value her opinion more than the teachers' for she knows about love and she knows that it is a thing which either does or does not exist. I think she knows more about love than anybody. I know that each time I've seen Marlene Dietrich she has touched my heart and made me happy. If that is what makes her mysterious, then mystery is a fine thing. And this mystery has been known to us for a long time.

FILMOGRAPHY

D Director
S Screenwriter
DP Director of photography
C Cast

The Little Napoleon 1923
Der kleine Napoleon or *So sind die Männer*
D Georg Jacoby
S Robert Liebman, Georg Jacoby
C Egon von Hagen, Paul Heidemann, Harry Liedtke, Jacob Tiedtke, Marlene Dietrich
Germany (Silent)

Tragedy of Love 1923
Tragödie der Liebe
D Joe May
S Leon Birinski, Adolf Lantz
DP Sophus Wangoe, Karl Putch
C Emil Jannings, Erika Glässner, Mia May, Kurt Vespermann, Marlene Dietrich
Germany (Silent)

Man by the Roadside 1923
Der Mensch am Wege
D Wilhelm Dieterle
S Wilhelm Dieterle (based on a novella by Leo Tolstoy)
DP Willy Hameister
C Alexander Granach, Wilhelm Dieterle, Heinrich George, Marlene Dietrich
Germany (Silent)

Leap into Life 1924
Der Sprung ins Leben
D Dr Johannes Guter
S Franz Schulz
DP Rudi Feldt
C Xenia Desni, Walter Rilla, Paul Heidemann, Frida Richard, Marlene Dietrich
Germany (Silent)

The Joyless Street (U.K.) or **The Street of Sorrow** (U.S.A.) 1925
Die freudlose Gasse
D Georg Wilhelm Pabst
S Willi Haas
DP Guido Seeber, Curt Oertel, Walter Robert Lach
C Jaro Furth, Greta Garbo, Asta Nielsen, Loni Nest, Silva Torf, Marlene Dietrich
Germany (Silent)

Manon Lescaut 1926
D Arthur Robison
S Hans Kyser, Arthur Robison
DP Theodor Sparkuhl
C Lya de Putti, Vladimir Gaidarov, Eduard Rothauser, Fritz Greiner, Marlene Dietrich
Germany (Silent)

A Modern Du Barry 1926
Eine Du Barry von Heute
D Alexander Korda
S Robert Liebmann, Alexander Korda, Paul Reboux
DP Fritz Arno Wagner
C Maria Corda, Alfred Abel, Friedrich Kayssler, Jean Bradin, Marlene Dietrich
Germany (Silent)

Madame Wants No Children 1926
Madame wünscht keine Kinder
D Alexander Korda
S Adolf Lantz, Bela Balazs (based on the novel by Clément Vautel)
DP Theodor Sparkuhl, Robert Baberske
C Maria Corda, Harry Liedtke, Maria Paudler, Trude Heisterberg, Marlene Dietrich
Germany (Silent)

Heads Up, Charlie! 1926
Kopf hoch, Charly!
D Dr Willi Wolff
S Robert Liebmann, Dr Willi Wolff
DP Axel Graatkjar
C Anton Pointner, Ellen Richter, Michael Bohnen, Max Gulsdorff, Marlene Dietrich
Germany (Silent)

The Imaginary Baron 1927
Der Juxbaron
D Dr Willi Wolff
S Robert Libemann, Dr Willi Wolff
DP Axel Graatkjar
C Reinhold Schunzel, Henry Bender, Julia Serda, Marlene Dietrich, Teddy Bill
Germany (Silent)

His Greatest Bluff 1927
Sein grösster Bluff
D Harry Piel
S Henrick Galeen
DP George Muschner, Gotthardt Wolf
C Harry Piel, Tony Tetzlaff, Lotte Lorring, Albert Paulig, Marlene Dietrich
Germany (Silent)

Café Electric 1927
Wenn ein Weib den Weg verliert
D Gustav Ucicky
S Jacques Bachrach
DP Hans Androschin
C Fritz Alberti, Marlene Dietrich, Anny Coty, Willi Forst, Igo Sym
Austria (Silent)

The Art of Love 1928
Prinzessin Olala
D Robert Land
S Franz Schulz, Robert Land (based on the operetta by Jean Gilbert)
DP Willi Goldberger
C Hermann Böttcher, Walter Rilla, Georg Alexander, Carmen Boni, Marlene Dietrich
Germany (Silent)

I Kiss Your Hand, Madame 1929
Ich küsse ihre Hand, Madame
D Robert Land
S Rolf E. Vanloo, Robert Land
DP Karl Drews, Gotthardt Wolf (assisted by Fred Zinnemann)
C Harry Liedtke, Marlene Dietrich, Pierre de Guingand, Karl Huszar-Puffy
Germany

Three Loves 1929
Die Frau, nach der man sich sehnt
D Kurt Bernhardt
S Ladislas Vajda (based on the novel by Max Brod)
DP Kurt Courant
C Marlene Dietrich, Fritz Kortner, Frida Richard, Oskar Sima, Uno Henning
Germany (Silent and sound version)

The Ship of Lost Men 1929
Das Schiff der verlorenen Menschen
D Maurice Tourneur (assisted by Jacques Tourneur)
S Maurice Tourneur (based on the novel by Frenzos Kerzemen)
DP Nikolaus Farkas
C Fritz Kortner, Marlene Dietrich, Gaston Modot, Robin Irvine, Vladimir Sokoloff
France, Germany (Silent)

Dangers of the Engagement Period 1929
Gefahren der Brautzeit
D Fred Sauer
S Walter Wassermann, Walter Schlee
DP Laszlo Schaffer
C Willi Forst, Marlene Dietrich, Lotte Lorring, Elza Temar, Bruno Ziener
Germany

The Blue Angel 1930
Der blaue Engel
D Josef von Sternberg
S Robert Liebmann, Carl Zuckmayer, Karl Vollmöller (based on the novel by Heinrich Mann, *Professor Unrath*)
DP Gunther Rittau, Hans Schneeberger
C Emil Jannings, Marlene Dietrich, Kurt Gerron, Rosa Valetti, Hans Albers
Germany

Morocco 1930
D Josef von Sternberg
S Jules Furthman (based on the novel by Benno Vigny *Amy Jolly*)
DP Lee Garmes
C Gary Cooper, Marlene Dietrich, Adolphe Menjou, Ulrich Haupt, Juliette Compton
U.S.A.

Dishonored 1931
D Josef von Sternberg
S Daniel H. Rubin (based on a story by Josef von Sternberg)
DP Lee Garmes
C Marlene Dietrich, Victor McLaglen, Lew Cody, Gustav von Seyffertitz
U.S.A.

Shanghai Express 1932
D Josef von Sternberg
S Jules Furthman (based on the novel by Harry Hervey)
DP Lee Garmes
C Marlene Dietrich, Clive Brook, Anna May Wong, Warner Oland, Eugene Palette
U.S.A.

Blonde Venus 1932
D Josef von Sternberg
S Jules Furthman, S.K. Lauren (based on a story by Josef von Sternberg)
DP Bert Glennon
C Marlene Dietrich, Herbert Marshall, Cary Grant, Dickie Moore, Gene Morgan
U.S.A.

Song of Songs 1933
D Rouben Mamoulian
S Leon Birinski, Samuel Hoffenstein (based on the novel by Hermann Sudermann)
DP Victor Milner
C Marlene Dietrich, Brian Aherne, Lionel Atwill, Alison Skipworth
U.S.A.

The Scarlet Empress 1934
D Josef von Sternberg
S Manuel Komroff (based on the diary kept by Catherine the Great)
DP Bert Glennon
C Marlene Dietrich, John Lodge, Sam Jaffe, Louise Dresser, Maria Sieber
U.S.A.

The Devil is a Woman 1935
D Josef von Sternberg
S John Dos Passos, S.K. Winston (based on the novel by Pierre Louÿs)
DP Josef von Sternberg, Lucien Ballard
C Marlene Dietrich, Lionel Atwill, Cesar Romero, Edward Everett Horton
U.S.A.

Desire 1936
D Frank Borzage
S Edwin Justus Mayer, Waldermar Young, Samuel Hoffenstein (based on the play by Hans Szekely and R.A. Stemmle)
DP Charles Lang
C Marlene Dietrich, Gary Cooper, John Halliday, William Frawley
U.S.A. (Film never completed)

I Loved a Soldier 1936
D Henry Hathaway
S John Van Druten
DP Charles Lang
C Marlene Dietrich, Charles Boyer, Akim Tamiroff, Walter Catlett
U.S.A.

The Garden of Allah 1936
D Richard Boleslawski
S W.P. Lipscomb, Lynn Rings (based on the novel by Robert Hichens)
DP W. Howard Greene
C Marlene Dietrich, Charles Boyer, Basil Rathbone, C. Aubrey Smith
U.S.A.

Knight Without Armour 1937
D Jacques Feyder
S Lajos Biro, Arthur Wimperis (based on the novel by James Hilton)
DP Harry Stradling
C Marlene Dietrich, Robert Donat, Irene Vanburgh, Herbert Lomas, Austin Trevor
U.K.

Angel 1937
D Ernst Lubitsch
S Sam Raphaelson (based on the play by Melchior Lengyell)
DP Charles Lange
C Marlene Dietrich, Herbert Marshall, Melvyn Douglas, Edward Everett Horton
U.S.A.

Destry Rides Again 1939
D George Marshall
S Felix Jackson, Henry Meyers, Gertrude Purcell (based on the novel by Max Brand)
DP Hal Mohr
C Marlene Dietrich, James Stewart, Charles Winninger, Mischa Auer
U.S.A.

Seven Sinners 1940
D Tay Garnett
S John Meeham, Harry Tugend (based on the novel by Ladislaus Fodor and Lazlo Vadnal)
DP Rudolph Mate
C Marlene Dietrich, John Wayne, Broderick Crawford, Mischa Auer, Albert Dekker
U.S.A.

The Flame of New Orleans 1941
D René Clair
S Norman Krasna
DP Rudolph Mate
C Marlene Dietrich, Bruce Cabot, Roland Young, Mischa Auer, Andy Devine
U.S.A.

Manpower 1941
D Raoul Walsh
S Richard Macaulay, Jerry Wald
C Edward G. Robinson, Marlene Dietrich, George Raft, Alan Hale, Frank McHugh
U.S.A.

The Lady is Willing 1942
D Mitchell Leisen
S James Edward Grant, Albert McCleery
DP Ted Tetzlaff
C Marlene Dietrich, Fred MacMurray, Aline MacMahon, Stanley Ridges
U.S.A.

The Spoilers 1942
D Ray Enright
S Lawrence Hazard, Tom Reed (based on the novel by Rex Beach)
DP Milton Krasner
C Marlene Dietrich, Randolph Scott, John Wayne, Margaret Lindsay
U.S.A.

Pittsburgh 1942
D Lewis Seiler
S Kenneth Gamet and Tom Reed (based on the novel by George Owen and Tom Reed)
DP Robert de Grasse
C Marlene Dietrich, Randolph Scott, John Wayne, Frank Craven, Louise Allbritton
U.S.A.

Follow the Boys 1944
D Eddie Sutherland
S Lou Breslow, Gertrude Purcell
DP David Abel
C George Raft, Vera Zorina, with appearances by Orson Welles, Marlene Dietrich, etc.
U.S.A.

Kismet 1944
D William Dieterle
S John Meehan (based on the play by Edward Knobloch)
DP Charles Rosher
C Ronald Colman, Marlene Dietrich, James Craig, Edward Arnold
U.S.A.

Martin Roumagnac 1946
D George Lacombe
S Pierre Véry (based on the novel by Pierre René Wolf)
DP Roger Hubert
C Marlene Dietrich, Jean Gabin, Margo Lion, Marcel Herrand, Daniel Gélin
France

Golden Earrings 1947
D Mitchell Leisen
S Abraham Polonski, Frank Butler, Helen Deutsch (based on the novel by Yolanda Foldes)
DP Daniel L. Fapp
C Ray Milland, Marlene Dietrich, Murvyn Vye, Bruce Lester, Reinhold Schunzel
U.S.A.

A Foreign Affair 1948
D Billy Wilder
S Charles Brackett, Billy Wilder, Richard L. Green (based on a story by David Shaw)
DP Charles B. Lang Jr
C Jean Arthur, Marlene Dietrich, John Lund, Millard Mitchell
U.S.A.

Jigsaw 1949
D Fletcher Markle
S Fletcher Markle, Vincent O'Connor (based on a story by John Roeburt)
DP Don Malkames
C Franchot Tone, Jean Wallace, Myron McCormick, with appearances by Henry Fonda, Marlene Dietrich, etc.
U.S.A.

Stage Fright 1950
D Alfred Hitchcock
S Whitfield Cook (based on the novel by Selwyn Jepson)
DP Wilkie Cooper
C Jane Wyman, Marlene Dietrich, Michael Wilding, Richard Todd, Alastair Sim
U.K.

No Highway (U.K.) or **No Highway in the Sky** (U.S.A.) 1951
D Henry Koster
S R.C. Sheriff, Oscar Millard, Alec Coppel (based on the novel by Nevil Shute)
DP Georges Perinal
C James Stewart, Marlene Dietrich, Glynis Johns, Jack Hawkins
U.K.

Rancho Notorious 1952
D Fritz Lang
S Daniel Taradash (based on the story by Sylvia Richard, *Gunshift Whitman*)
DP Hal Mohr
C Marlene Dietrich, Arthur Kennedy, Mel Ferrer, Lloyd Gough, Gloria Henry
U.S.A.

Around the World in Eighty Days 1956
D Michael Anderson
S James Poe, John Farrow, S.J. Perelman (based on the novel by Jules Verne)
DP Lionel Lindon
C David Niven, Cantinflas, Robert Newton, Shirley MacLaine, with appearances by Charles Boyer, Marlene Dietrich etc.
U.S.A.

The Monte Carlo Story 1957
D Samuel A. Taylor
S Samuel A. Taylor (based on the story by Marcello Girosi and Dino Rosi)
DP Giuseppe Rotunno
C Marlene Dietrich, Vittorio de Sica, Arthur O'Connell, Natalie Trundy
Italy

Witness for the Prosecution 1958
D Billy Wilder
S Harry Kurnitz, Billy Wilder (based on the play by Agatha Christie)
DP Russell Harlan
C Tyrone Power, Marlene Dietrich, Charles Laughton, Elsa Lanchester
U.K.

Touch of Evil 1958
D Orson Welles
S Orson Welles (based on the novel by Whit Masterson, *Badge of Evil*)
DP Russell Metty
C Charlton Heston, Janet Leigh, Orson Welles, with appearances by Marlene Dietrich and Zsa Zsa Gabor
U.S.A.

Judgment at Nuremberg 1961
D Stanley Kramer
S Abby Mann
DP Ernest Laszlo
C Spencer Tracy, Burt Lancaster, Richard Widmark, Marlene Dietrich, Maximilian Schell, Judy Garland, Montgomery Clift
U.S.A.

Black Fox 1962
D Louis Clyde Stoumen
S Louis Clyde Stoumen
Documentary Narration by Marlene Dietrich
U.S.A.

Paris When it Sizzles 1964
D Richard Quine
S George Axelrod
DP Charles B. Lang Jr
C William Holden, Audrey Hepburn, Grégoire Aslan, Noël Coward, with an appearance by Marlene Dietrich
U.S.A.

Just a Gigolo 1978
D David Hemmings
C David Bowie, Kim Novak, with an appearance by Marlene Dietrich
U.K./Germany

THE SONGS FROM MARLENE'S FILMS

The Blue Angel
'Nimm dich in Acht vor blonden Frauen' (*Frederick Hollander–Robert Liebmann*)
'Ich bin die fesche Lola' (*Frederick Hollander–Robert Liebmann*)
'Kinder, heut' Abend such ich mir was aus' (*Frederick Hollander–Robert Liebmann*)
'Ich bin von Kopf bis Fuss auf Liebe eingestellt' (Falling in love again) (*Frederick Hollander–Robert Liebmann*)

Morocco
'Give Me the Man' (*Leon Robin–Karl Hajos*)
'What Am I Bid?' (*Leo Robin–Karl Hajos*)
'Quand l'amour meurt' (*Millandy–Crémieux*)

Blonde Venus
'Hot Voodoo' (*Sam Coslow–Ralph Rainger*)
'You Little So-and-so' (*Sam Coslow–Ralph Rainger*)
'I Couldn't Be So Annoyed' (*Leo Robin–Dick Whiting*)

Song of Songs
'Johnny' (*Frederick Hollander–Edward Heymann*)

The Devil is a Woman
'If It isn't Pain, then It isn't Love' (*Leo Robin–Ralph Rainger*)
'Three Sweethearts Have I' (*Leo Robin–Ralph Rainger*)

Desire
'Awake in a Dream' (*Frederick Hollander–Leo Robin*)

Destry Rides Again
'Little Joe the Wrangler' (*Frederick Hollander–Frank Loesser*)
'You've Got That Look That Leaves Me Weak (*Frederick Hollander–Frank Loesser*)
'The Boys in the Back Room' (*Frederick Hollander–Frank Loesser*)

Seven Sinners
'I've Been in Love Before' (*Frederick Hollander–Frank Loesser*)
'I Fall Overboard' (*Frederick Hollander–Frank Loesser*)
'The Man's in the Navy' (*Frederick Hollander–Frank Loesser*)

The Flame of New Orleans
'Sweet as the Blush of May' (*Charles Previn–Sam Lerner*)

Manpower
'I'm in No Mood for Music Tonight' (*Frederick Hollander–Frank Loesser*)
'He Lied and I Listened (*Frederick Hollander–Frank Loesser*)

The Lady is Willing
'Strange Thing, and I Find You' (*Jack King–Gordon Clifford*)

Kismet
'Willow in the Wind' (*Harold Arlen–E.Y. Harburg*)
'Tell Me, Tell Me, Evening Star' (*Harold Arlen–E.Y. Harburg*)

Golden Earrings
'Golden Earrings' (*Victor Young–Jay Livingstone–Ray Evans*)

A Foreign Affair
'Black Market' (*Frederick Hollander*)
'Illusions' (*Frederick Hollander*)
'Ruins of Berlin' (*Frederick Hollander*)

Stage Fright
'The Laziest Gal in Town' (*Cole Porter*)
'La Vie en Rose' (*Edith Piaf–Louiguy*)

Rancho Notorious
'Gypsy, Davey' (*Ken Darby*)
'Get Away, Young Man' (*Ken Darby*)

The Monte Carlo Story
'Les Jeux sont Faits' (*Michel Emer*)
'Rien ne va plus' (*Michel Emer*)
'My Indiana Home' (*Michel Emer*)

Witness for the Prosecution
'I May Never Go Home Anymore' (*Ralph A. Roberts–Jack Brooks*)

BIBLIOGRAPHY

Marlene Dietrich, *Nehmt nur mein Leben*, Bertelsmann/Goldmann RFA, Munich, 1979.

Marlene Dietrich, *Marlene Dietrich's ABC*, Doubleday and Company, New York, 1962.

Josef von Sternberg, *Fun in a Chinese Laundry*, Secker and Warburg, London, 1965.

Josef von Sternberg, *Morocco/Shanghai Express*, Lorrimer Publishers, London, 1972.

INDEX

Page numbers in italics refer to illustrations